CEOE OSAT
Field 26
Middle Level Science
Teacher Certification Exam

By: Sharon Wynne, M.S
Southern Connecticut State University

"And, while there's no reason yet to panic, I think it's only prudent that we make preparations to panic."

XAMonline, INC.
Boston

Copyright © 2007 XAMonline, Inc.

All rights reserved. No part of the material protected by this copyright notice may be reproduced or utilized in any form or by any means, electronic or mechanical, including photocopying, recording or by any information storage and retrievable system, without written permission from the copyright holder.

To obtain permission(s) to use the material from this work for any purpose including workshops or seminars, please submit a written request to:

XAMonline, Inc.
21 Orient Ave.
Melrose, MA 02176
Toll Free 1-800-509-4128
Email: info@xamonline.com
Web www.xamonline.com
Fax: 1-781-662-9268

Library of Congress Cataloging-in-Publication Data

Wynne, Sharon A.
 OSAT Middle Level Science Field 26: Teacher Certification / Sharon A. Wynne. -2nd ed.
 ISBN 978-1-58197-789-9
  1. OSAT Middle Level Science Field 26.   2. Study Guides.   3. CEOE
  4. Teachers' Certification & Licensure.   5. Careers

Disclaimer:

The opinions expressed in this publication are the sole works of XAMonline and were created independently from the National Education Association, Educational Testing Service, or any State Department of Education, National Evaluation Systems or other testing affiliates.

Between the time of publication and printing, state specific standards as well as testing formats and website information may change that is not included in part or in whole within this product. Sample test questions are developed by XAMonline and reflect similar content as on real tests; however, they are not former tests. XAMonline assembles content that aligns with state standards but makes no claims nor guarantees teacher candidates a passing score. Numerical scores are determined by testing companies such as NES or ETS and then are compared with individual state standards. A passing score varies from state to state.

Printed in the United States of America œ-1

CEOE: OSAT Middle Level Science Field 26
ISBN: 978-1-58197-789-9

TEACHER CERTIFICATION STUDY GUIDE

Table of Contents

SUBAREA I. FOUNDATIONS OF SCIENTIFIC INQUIRY

COMPETENCY 1.0 UNDERSTAND THE RELATIONSHIPS AND COMMON THEMES THAT CONNECT MATHEMATICS, SCIENCE, AND TECHNOLOGY 1

Skill 1.1 Identify distinguishing characteristics of mathematics, science, and technology 1

Skill 1.2 Analyze the relationships between science, mathematics, and technology 2

Skill 1.3 Recognize the role of models in science, mathematics, and technology 2

Skill 1.4 Identify general concepts common to mathematics, science, and technology 4

COMPETENCY 2.0 UNDERSTAND THE HISTORICAL AND CONTEMPORARY CONTEXTS OF THE STUDY OF SCIENCE 5

Skill 2.1 Analyze the significance of key events, theories, experiments, and individuals in the history of science 5

Skill 2.2 Identify the scientific contributions of individuals and societies of different periods and cultures 7

Skill 2.3 Analyze the role of science in daily life 8

MID. LEVEL SCIENCE

TEACHER CERTIFICATION STUDY GUIDE

COMPETENCY 3.0   **UNDERSTAND THE PROCESSES OF SCIENTIFIC INQUIRY AND THE ROLE OF OBSERVATION AND EXPERIMENTATION IN EXPLAINING AND/OR PREDICTING NATURAL PHENOMENA 9**

Skill 3.1   Identify appropriate questions to ask in a given scientific context 9

Skill 3.2   Identify processes by which new scientific knowledge and hypotheses are generated 10

Skill 3.3   Evaluate the appropriateness of a given experimental design to test a hypothesis 11

Skill 3.4   Analyze ethical issues related to the process of scientific inquiry 12

COMPETENCY 4.0   **UNDERSTAND PRINCIPLES OF MEASUREMENT AND THE PROCESSES OF GATHERING, ORGANIZING, REPORTING, AND INTERPRETING SCIENTIFIC DATA 13**

Skill 4.1   Identify procedures for gathering and collecting relevant and reliable data in a given situation 13

Skill 4.2   Analyze procedures and formats used in organizing, interpreting, and reporting data 13

Skill 4.3   Solve problems involving measurements and units of measure 14

COMPETENCY 5.0   **UNDERSTAND THE USE OF EQUIPMENT, MATERIALS, AND CHEMICALS IN SCIENTIFIC INQUIRY; AND APPLY PROCEDURES FOR THEIR PROPER, SAFE, AND LEGAL USE 15**

Skill 5.1   Apply procedures for selecting and safely using common laboratory equipment 15

Skill 5.2   Identify procedures for the safe storage, use, and disposal of common laboratory chemicals 16

Skill 5.3   Identify procedures for the proper and humane treatment and safe handling of classroom animals 17

Skill 5.4   Apply procedures for promoting laboratory safety and appropriately responding to accidents and injuries in the science laboratory 17

TEACHER CERTIFICATION STUDY GUIDE

SUBAREA II.	LIFE SCIENCE

COMPETENCY 6.0 UNDERSTAND BASIC CONCEPTS OF CELL BIOLOGY 19

Skill 6.1 Identify the components and principles of the cell theory 19

Skill 6.2 Recognize basic cell structures and their functions 20

Skill 6.3 Compare the structure of animal and plant cells 22

Skill 6.4 Identify the role of organic molecules in cells and organisms 23

COMPETENCY 7.0 UNDERSTAND CHARACTERISTICS OF LIFE AND BASIC LIFE PROCESS 25

Skill 7.1 Recognize differences between organisms and nonliving things 25

Skill 7.2 Identify the characteristics of major groups of organisms 25

Skill 7.3 Analyze the processes of photosynthesis and cellular respiration 27

Skill 7.4 Analyze basic life processes 28

Skill 7.5 Identify the structure, components, functions, and physiological processes of organs and systems in plants and animals 29

COMPETENCY 8.0 UNDERSTAND GENETICS AND BIOLOGICAL ADAPTATION 31

Skill 8.1 Identify the structure and function of genes and chromosomes 31

Skill 8.2 Analyze processes by which characteristics are passed on 31

Skill 8.3 Analyze the roles of variation, natural selection, and adaptation in biological evolution 34

MID. LEVEL SCIENCE

TEACHER CERTIFICATION STUDY GUIDE

COMPETENCY 9.0   **UNDERSTAND POPULATIONS, COMMUNITIES, ECOSYSTEMS, AND BIOMES** **36**

Skill 9.1   Identify the characteristics of populations, communities, ecosystems, and biomes 36

Skill 9.2   Analyze factors that affect population growth and community interactions 37

Skill 9.3   Analyze the movement of energy and materials through the trophic levels of an ecosystem 40

COMPETENCY 10.0   **UNDERSTAND THE EFFECT OF HUMANS ON THE ENVIRONMENT** **41**

Skill 10.1   Identify sources of environmental pollutants 41

Skill 10.2   Analyze the effects of humans on natural processes and environments 42

Skill 10.3   Analyze techniques and procedures for protecting the environment 43

MID. LEVEL SCIENCE

TEACHER CERTIFICATION STUDY GUIDE

SUBAREA III.   PHYSICAL SCIENCE

COMPETENCY 11.0   UNDERSTAND THE STRUCTURE AND NATURE OF MATTER 44

Skill 11.1   Identify the parts of an atom and their characteristics 44

Skill 11.2   Identify the physical and chemical characteristics of matter 45

Skill 11.2   Recognize types and characteristics of chemical bonding and its relationship to molecular structures 47

Skill 11.3   Use the kinetic molecular model, the periodic table of the elements, and other models of atomic structure to explain and predict the behavior of matter 48

COMPETENCY 12.0   UNDERSTAND PHYSICAL AND CHEMICAL CHANGES AND CHEMICAL REACTIONS 50

Skill 12.1   Distinguish between physical and chemical changes and their characteristics 50

Skill 12.2   Analyze types of chemical reactions and their characteristics 50

Skill 12.3   Interpret notation used to represent chemical reactions 51

COMPETENCY 13.0   UNDERSTAND THE BASIC CONCEPTS OF FORCE, WORK, AND MOTION 52

Skill 13.1   Identify types and characteristics of force, work, and motion 52

Skill 13.2   Identify the forces affecting an object in a given situation 53

Skill 13.3   Apply physical laws to interpret and predict the motion of objects 54

MID. LEVEL SCIENCE

COMPETENCY 14.0 UNDERSTAND ENERGY AND ITS FORMS AND TRANSFORMATIONS 57

Skill 14.1 Identify forms of energy and their characteristics 57

Skill 14.2 Recognize the conservation of energy in various situations 57

Skill 14.3 Identify and analyze energy transfers and conversions 58

Skill 14.4 Recognize the relationship between kinetic and potential energy 59

COMPETENCY 15.0 UNDERSTAND WAVES, SOUND, AND LIGHT 60

Skill 15.1 Use terms associated with waves, sound, and light 60

Skill 15.2 Identify phenomena related to waves, sound, and light 60

Skill 15.3 Analyze given situations in terms of the behavior of waves, sound, and light 61

COMPETENCY 16.0 UNDERSTAND ELECTRICITY, MAGNETS, AND ELECTROMAGNETISM 63

Skill 16.1 Identify the characteristics of static electricity, current electricity, and electric circuits 63

Skill 16.2 Analyze the relationship between electricity and magnetism 63

Skill 16.3 Demonstrate knowledge of the characteristics of magnets and magnetic fields 64

TEACHER CERTIFICATION STUDY GUIDE

SUBAREA IV.   **EARTH AND SPACE SCIENCE**

COMPETENCY 17.0   UNDERSTAND GEOLOGY AND GEOLOGIC HISTORY 65

Skill 17.1   Identify characteristics of rocks, minerals, and soils and the processes by which they form 65

Skill 17.2   Identify the structure and composition of the earth and the interactions among its layers 66

Skill 17.3   Analyze processes that produce geologic change and transformation 68

Skill 17.4   Interpret maps commonly used in earth science 71

Skill 17.5   Identify the ecological impact of geologic events 73

COMPETENCY 18.0   UNDERSTAND WATER AND THE HYDROSPHERE 75

Skill 18.1   Identify characteristics of freshwater and saltwater 75

Skill 18.2   Identify characteristics and effects of the water cycle 76

Skill 18.2   Recognize factors that affect the movement of surface water and groundwater 77

Skill 18.3   Identify factors that affect the biological productivity of bodies of water 81

COMPETENCY 19.0 UNDERSTAND WEATHER, CLIMATE, AND THE EARTH'S ATMOSPHERE 82

Skill 19.1   Identify the structure, functions, and characteristics of the earth's atmosphere 82

Skill 19.2   Analyze the role of air masses and their movements in affecting weather 83

Skill 19.3   Recognize processes related to precipitation and cloud formation 84

Skill 19.4   Analyze the use of maps, equipment, and techniques in predicting and interpreting weather and climatic changes 85

Skill 19.5   Identify the effects of weather events and climatic changes on ecosystems 86

COMPETENCY 20.0 UNDERSTAND BASIC ASTRONOMY 88

Skill 20.1   Analyze theories of the structure, origin, and evolution of the solar system and universe 88

Skill 20.2   Identify the components of the solar system and their characteristics, interactions, and movements 89

Skill 20.3   Identify the characteristics of stars and galaxies 92

Skill 20.4   Recognize the significance and advancement of space exploration and its impact on society 94

Sample Test 95

Answer Key 118

Sample Questions with Rationale 119

TEACHER CERTIFICATION STUDY GUIDE

Great Study and Testing Tips!

What to study in order to prepare for the subject assessments is the focus of this study guide but equally important is *how* you study.

You can increase your chances of truly mastering the information by taking some simple, but effective steps.

Study Tips:

1. Some foods aid the learning process. Foods such as milk, nuts, seeds, rice, and oats help your study efforts by releasing natural memory enhancers called CCKs (*cholecystokinin*) composed of *tryptophan*, *choline*, and *phenylalanine*. All of these chemicals enhance the neurotransmitters associated with memory. Before studying, try a light, protein-rich meal of eggs, turkey, and fish. All of these foods release the memory enhancing chemicals. The better the connections, the more you comprehend.

Likewise, before you take a test, stick to a light snack of energy boosting and relaxing foods. A glass of milk, a piece of fruit, or some peanuts all release various memory-boosting chemicals and help you to relax and focus on the subject at hand.

2. Learn to take great notes. A by-product of our modern culture is that we have grown accustomed to getting our information in short doses (i.e. TV news sound bites or USA Today style newspaper articles.)

Consequently, we've subconsciously trained ourselves to assimilate information better in neat little packages. If your notes are scrawled all over the paper, it fragments the flow of the information. Strive for clarity. Newspapers use a standard format to achieve clarity. Your notes can be much clearer through use of proper formatting. A very effective format is called *"Cornell Method."*

> Take a sheet of loose-leaf lined notebook paper and draw a line all the way down the paper about 1-2" from the left-hand edge.
>
> Draw another line across the width of the paper about 1-2" up from the bottom. Repeat this process on the reverse side of the page.

Look at the highly effective result. You have ample room for notes, a left hand margin for special emphasis items or inserting supplementary data from the textbook, a large area at the bottom for a brief summary, and a little rectangular space for just about anything you want.

3. **Get the concept then the details.** Too often we focus on the details and don't gather an understanding of the concept. However, if you simply memorize only dates, places, or names, you may well miss the whole point of the subject.

A key way to understand things is to put them in your own words. If you are working from a textbook, automatically summarize each paragraph in your mind. If you are outlining text, don't simply copy the author's words.

Rephrase them in your own words. You remember your own thoughts and words much better than someone else's, and subconsciously tend to associate the important details to the core concepts.

4. **Ask Why?** Pull apart written material paragraph by paragraph and don't forget the captions under the illustrations.

Example: If the heading is "Stream Erosion", flip it around to read "Why do streams erode?" Then answer the questions.

If you train your mind to think in a series of questions and answers, not only will you learn more, but it also helps to lessen the test anxiety because you are used to answering questions.

5. **Read for reinforcement and future needs.** Even if you only have 10 minutes, put your notes or a book in your hand. Your mind is similar to a computer; you have to input data in order to have it processed. *By reading, you are creating the neural connections for future retrieval.* The more times you read something, the more you reinforce the learning of ideas.

Even if you don't fully understand something on the first pass, *your mind stores much of the material for later recall.*

6. **Relax to learn so go into exile.** Our bodies respond to an inner clock called biorhythms. Burning the midnight oil works well for some people, but not everyone.

If possible, set aside a particular place to study that is free of distractions. Shut off the television, cell phone, pager and exile your friends and family during your study period.

If you really are bothered by silence, try background music. Light classical music at a low volume has been shown to aid in concentration over other types. Music that evokes pleasant emotions without lyrics are highly suggested. Try just about anything by Mozart. It relaxes you.

MID. LEVEL SCIENCE

7. Use arrows not highlighters. At best, it's difficult to read a page full of yellow, pink, blue, and green streaks. Try staring at a neon sign for a while and you'll soon see that the horde of colors obscure the message.

A quick note, a brief dash of color, an underline, and an arrow pointing to a particular passage is much clearer than a horde of highlighted words.

8. Budget your study time. Although you shouldn't ignore any of the material, *allocate your available study time in the same ratio that topics may appear on the test.*

Testing Tips:

1. Get smart, play dumb. Don't read anything into the question. Don't make an assumption that the test writer is looking for something else than what is asked. Stick to the question as written and don't read extra things into it.

2. Read the question and all the choices *twice* before answering the question. You may miss something by not carefully reading, and then re-reading both the question and the answers.

If you really don't have a clue as to the right answer, leave it blank on the first time through. Go on to the other questions, as they may provide a clue as to how to answer the skipped questions.

If later on, you still can't answer the skipped ones . . . **Guess.** The only penalty for guessing is that you *might* get it wrong. Only one thing is certain; if you don't put anything down, you will get it wrong!

3. Turn the question into a statement. Look at the way the questions are worded. The syntax of the question usually provides a clue. Does it seem more familiar as a statement rather than as a question? Does it sound strange?

By turning a question into a statement, you may be able to spot if an answer sounds right, and it may also trigger memories of material you have read.

4. Look for hidden clues. It's actually very difficult to compose multiple-foil (choice) questions without giving away part of the answer in the options presented.

In most multiple-choice questions you can often readily eliminate one or two of the potential answers. This leaves you with only two real possibilities and automatically your odds go to Fifty-Fifty for very little work.

5. Trust your instincts. For every fact that you have read, you subconsciously retain something of that knowledge. On questions that you aren't really certain about, go with your basic instincts. **Your first impression on how to answer a question is usually correct.**

6. Mark your answers directly on the test booklet. Don't bother trying to fill in the optical scan sheet on the first pass through the test.

Just be very careful not to miss-mark your answers when you eventually transcribe them to the scan sheet.

7. Watch the clock! You have a set amount of time to answer the questions. Don't get bogged down trying to answer a single question at the expense of 10 questions you can more readily answer.

MID. LEVEL SCIENCE

TEACHER CERTIFICATION STUDY GUIDE

SUBAREA I. FOUNDATIONS OF SCIENTIFIC INQUIRY

COMPETENCY 1.0 UNDERSTAND THE RELATIONSHIPS AND COMMON THEMES THAT CONNECT MATHEMATICS, SCIENCE, AND TECHNOLOGY

Skill 1.1 Identify distinguishing characteristics of mathematics, science, and technology

A synergistic relationship exists among basic and applied research, mathematics, and technology. Basic research is the starting point in this chain of events. When assessing scientific information, scientists often use mathematics. Many chemical processes can be evaluated using formulas and statistics, and instruments require calibration, which is also a utilization of mathematics. Science depends on data and the manipulation of data requires knowledge of mathematics. Understanding of basic statistics, graphs and charts, and algebra are of particular importance. Scientists must be able to understand and apply the statistical concepts of mean, median, mode, and range to sets of scientific data. In addition, scientists must be able to represent data graphically and interpret graphs and tables. Finally, scientists often use basic algebra to solve scientific problems and design experiments. Basic research provides knowledge. The first type of knowledge is theoretical knowledge, giving us the understanding of processes. The second type of knowledge could be applied for the benefit of humanity. Applied research is of great value because it is directly useful to us; it deals with issues like AIDS, Tuberculosis, HPV, Parkinson's disease, etc. The public is interested in these issues and has its opinions about research, sometimes leading to controversy. Technology fulfills a human need, and is often reliant upon scientific research.

Skill 1.2   Analyze the relationships between science, mathematics, and technology

Science and technology are interdependent as advances in technology often lead to new scientific discoveries and new scientific discoveries often lead to new technologies. Scientists use technology to enhance the study of nature and solve problems that nature presents. Technological design is the identification of a problem and the application of scientific knowledge to solve the problem. Scientific disciplines share several unifying concepts and processes that help unify the study of science. Science and technology, while distinct concepts, are closely related. Science attempts to investigate and explain the natural world, while technology attempts to solve human adaptation problems. Technology often results from the application of scientific discoveries, and advances in technology can increase the impact of scientific discoveries. The combination of biology and technology has improved the human standard of living in many ways. However, the negative impact of increasing human life expectancy and population on the environment is problematic. In addition, advances in biotechnology (e.g. genetic engineering, cloning) produce ethical dilemmas that society must consider.

Skill 1.3   Recognize the role of models (e.g., scale models, simulations, formulas) in science, mathematics, and technology

The model is a basic element of the scientific method. Many things in science are studied with models. A model is any simplification or substitute for what we are actually studying, understanding or predicting. A model is a substitute, but it is similar to what it represents. We encounter models at every step of our daily living. The Periodic Table of the elements is a model chemists use for predicting the properties of the elements. Physicists use Newton's laws to predict how objects will interact, such as planets and spaceships. In geology, the continental drift model predicts the past positions of continents. Sample, ideas, and methods are all examples of models. At every step of scientific study, models are extensively use. The primary activity of the hundreds of thousands of US scientists is to produce new models, resulting in tens of thousands of scientific papers published per year.

Types of models:

* Scale models: some models are basically downsized or enlarged copies of their target systems like the models of protein, DNA, etc.
* Idealized models: An idealization is a deliberate simplification of something complicated with the objective of making it easier to understand. Some examples are frictionless planes, point masses, isolated systems, etc.
* Analogical models: standard examples of analogical models are the billiard model of a gas, the computer model of the mind, or the liquid drop model of the nucleus.
*Phenomenological models: These are usually defined as models that are independent of theories.
*Data models: It s a corrected, rectified, regimented, and in many instances, idealized version of the data we gain from immediate observation (raw data).
*Theory models: Any structure is a model if it represents an idea (theory). An example of this is a flow chart, which summarizes a set of ideas.

Uses of models:

1. Models are crucial for understanding the structure and function of processes in science.
2. Models help us to visualize the organs/systems they represent just like putting a face to a person.
3. Models are very useful to predict and foresee future events like hurricanes, etc.

Limitations:

1. Though models are every useful to us, they can never replace the real thing.
2. Models are not exactly like the real item they represent.
3. Caution must be exercised before presenting the models to the class, as they may not be accurate.
4. It is the responsibility of the educator to analyze the model critically for the proportions, content value, and other important data.
5. One must be careful about the representation style. This style differs from person to person.

Skill 1.4   **Identify general concepts common to mathematics, science, and technology (e.g., order, scale, modeling, cause and effect, systems, constancy)**

The following are the concepts and processes generally recognized as common to all scientific disciplines:

Systems, order, and organization
Because the natural world is so complex, the study of science involves the **organization** of items into smaller groups based on interaction or interdependence. These groups are called **systems**. Examples of organization are the periodic table of elements and the five-kingdom classification scheme for living organisms. Examples of systems are the solar system, cardiovascular system, Newton's laws of force and motion, and the laws of conservation. **Order** refers to the behavior and measurability of organisms and events in nature. The arrangement of planets in the solar system and the life cycle of bacterial cells are examples of order.

Evidence, models, and explanations
Scientists use **evidence** and **models** to form **explanations** of natural events. Models are miniaturized representations of a larger event or system. Evidence is anything that furnishes proof.

Constancy, change, and measurement
Constancy and **change** describe the observable properties of natural organisms and events. Scientists use different systems of **measurement** to observe change and constancy. For example, the freezing and melting points of given substances and the speed of sound are constant under constant conditions. Growth, decay, and erosion are all examples of natural change.

Evolution and equilibrium
Evolution is the process of change over a long period of time. While biological evolution is the most common example, one can also classify technological advancement, changes in the universe, and changes in the environment as evolution.
Equilibrium is the state of balance between opposing forces of change. Homeostasis and ecological balance are examples of equilibrium.

Form and function
Form and **function** are properties of organisms and systems that are closely related. The function of an object usually dictates its form and the form of an object usually facilitates its function. For example, the form of the heart (e.g. muscle, valves) allows it to perform its function of circulating blood through the body.

COMPETENCY 2.0 UNDERSTAND THE HISTORICAL AND CONTEMPORARY CONTEXTS OF THE STUDY OF SCIENCE

Skill 2.1 Analyze the significance of key events, theories, experiments, and individuals in the history of science

The history of biology traces mans' understanding of the living world from the earliest recorded history to modern times. Though the concept of biology as a field of science arose only in the 19th century, the origin of biological sciences could be traced back to ancient Greeks (Galen and Aristotle).

During the Renaissance and Age of Discovery, renewed interest in the rapidly increasing number of known organisms generated lot of interest in biology.

Andreas Vesalius (1514-1564) was a Belgian anatomist and physician whose dissections of human body and descriptions of his findings helped to correct the misconceptions of science. The books Vesalius wrote on anatomy were the most accurate and comprehensive anatomical texts to date.

Anton van Leeuwenhoek is known as the father of microscopy. In the 1650s, Leeuwenhoek began making tiny lenses that gave magnifications up to 300x. He was the first to see and describe bacteria, yeast plants, and the microscopic life found in water. Over the years, light microscopes have advanced to produce greater clarity and magnification. The scanning electron microscope (SEM) was developed in the 1950s. Instead of light, a beam of electrons passes through the specimen. Scanning electron microscopes have a resolution about one thousand times greater than light microscopes. The disadvantage of the SEM is that the chemical and physical methods used to prepare the sample result in the death of the specimen.

Robert Hooke (1635-1703) was a renowned inventor, a natural philosopher, astronomer, experimenter and a cell biologist. He deserves more recognition than he had, but he is remembered mainly for his law, the Hooke's law—an equation describing elasticity that is still used today. He was the type of scientist that was then called a "virtuoso"- able to contribute findings of major importance in any field of science. Hooke published *Micrographia* in 1665. Hooke devised the compound microscope and illumination system, one of the best such microscopes of his time, and used it in his demonstrations at the Royal Society's meetings. With it, he observed organisms as diverse as insects, sponges, bryozoans, foraminifera, and bird feathers. Micrographia is an accurate and detailed record of his observations, illustrated with magnificent drawings.

Carl Von Linnaeus (1707-1778), a Swedish botanist, physician and zoologist is well known for his contributions in ecology and taxonomy. Linnaeus is famous for his binomial system of nomenclature in which each living organism has two names, a genus and a species name. He is considered as the father of modern ecology and taxonomy.

In the late 1800s, Pasteur discovered the role of microorganisms in the cause of disease, pasteurization, and the rabies vaccine. Koch took this observations one step further by formulating that specific diseases were caused by specific pathogens. **Koch's postulates** are still used as guidelines in the field of microbiology: the same pathogen must be found in every diseased person, the pathogen must be isolated and grown in culture, the disease is induced in experimental animals from the culture, and the same pathogen must be isolated from the experimental animal.

Mattias Schleiden, a German botanist is famous for his cell theory. He observed plant cells microscopically and concluded that cell is the common structural unit of plants. He proposed the cell theory along with Schwann, a zoologist, who observed cells in animals.

In the 18th century, many fields of science like botany, zoology and geology began to evolve as scientific disciplines in the modern sense.

In the 20th century, the rediscovery of Mendel's work led to the rapid development of genetics by Thomas Hunt Morgan and his students.

DNA structure was another key event in biological study. In the 1950s, James Watson and Francis Crick discovered the structure of a DNA molecule as that of a double helix. This structure made it possible to explain DNA's ability to replicate and to control the synthesis of proteins.

Francois Jacob and Jacques Monod contributed greatly to the field of lysogeny and bacterial reproduction by conjugation and both of them won Nobel Prize for their contributions.

Following the cracking of the genetic code, biology has largely split between organismal biology consisting of ecology, ethology, systematics, paleontology, evolutionary biology, developmental biology, and other disciplines that deal with whole organisms or groups of organisms and the disciplines related to molecular biology - including cell biology, biophysics, biochemistry, neuroscience, immunology, and many other overlapping subjects.

The use of animals in biological research has expedited many scientific discoveries. Animal research has allowed scientists to learn more about animal biological systems, including the circulatory and reproductive systems. One significant use of animals is for the testing of drugs, vaccines, and other products (such as perfumes and shampoos) before use or consumption by humans. Along with the pros of animal research, the cons are also very significant. The debate about the ethical treatment of animals has been ongoing since the introduction of animals in research. Many people believe the use of animals in research is cruel and unnecessary. Animal use is federally and locally regulated. The purpose of the Institutional Animal Care and Use Committee (IACUC) is to oversee and evaluate all aspects of an institution's animal care and use program.

Skill 2.2   Identify the scientific contributions of individuals and societies of different periods and cultures

Curiosity is the heart of science. Maybe this is why so many diverse people are drawn to it. In the area of zoology one of the most recognized scientists is Jane Goodall. Miss Goodall is known for her research with chimpanzees in Africa. Jane has spent many years abroad conducting long-term studies of chimp interactions, and returns from Africa to lecture and provide information about Africa, the chimpanzees, and her institute located in Tanzania.

In the area of chemistry we recognize Dorothy Crowfoot Hodgkin. She studied at Oxford and won the Nobel Prize of Chemistry in 1964 for recognizing the shape of the vitamin B 12.

Have you ever heard of Florence Nightingale? She was a true person living in the 1800's and she shaped the nursing profession. Florence was born into wealth and shocked her family by choosing to study health reforms for the poor in lieu of attending the expected social events. Florence studied nursing in Paris and became involved in the Crimean war. The British lacked supplies and the secretary of war asked for Florence's assistance. She earned her nickname walking the floors at night checking on patients and writing letters to British officials demanding supplies.

In 1903, the Nobel Prize in Physics was jointly awarded to three individuals: Marie Curie, Pierre Curie, and Becquerel. Marie was the first woman ever to receive this prestigious award. In addition, she received the Nobel Prize in chemistry in 1911, making her the only person to receive two Nobel awards in science. Ironically, her cause of death in 1934 was of overexposure to radioactivity, the research for which she was so respected.

Neil Armstrong is an American icon. He will always be symbolically linked to our aeronautics program. This astronaut and naval aviator is known for being the first human to set foot on the Moon.

Sir Alexander Flemming was a pharmacologist from Scotland who isolated the antibiotic penicillin from a fungus in 1928. Flemming also noted that bacteria developed resistance whenever too little penicillin was used or when it was used for too short a period, a key problem we still face today.

It is important to realize that many of the most complex scientific questions have been answered in a collaborative form. The human genome project is a great example of research conducted and shared by multiple countries world wide. It is also interesting to note that because of differing cultural beliefs, some cultures may be more likely to allow areas of research that other cultures may be unlikely to examine.

The goal of the human genome project is to map and sequence the three billion nucleotides in the human genome, and to identify all of the genes on it. The project was launched in 1986 and an outline of the genome was finished in 2000 through international collaboration. In May 2006, the sequence of the last chromosome was published. While the map and sequencing are complete, scientists are still studying the functions of all the genes and their regulation. Humans have successfully decoded the genome of other mammals as well.

Skill 2.3   Analyze the role of science in daily life.

Because biology is the study of living things, we can easily apply the knowledge of biology and other scientific disciplines to daily life and personal decision-making. For example, biology greatly influences the health decisions humans make everyday. What foods to eat, when and how to exercise, and how often to bathe are just three of the many decisions we make everyday that are based on our knowledge of biology. Other areas of daily life where biology affects decision-making are parenting, interpersonal relationships, family planning, and consumer spending.

COMPETENCY 3.0 UNDERSTAND THE PROCESSES OF SCIENTIFIC INQUIRY AND THE ROLE OF OBSERVATION AND EXPERIMENTATION IN EXPLAINING AND/OR PREDICTING NATURAL PHENOMENA

Skill 3.1 Identify appropriate questions to ask in a given scientific context

Only certain types of questions can truly be answered by science because the scientific method relies on observable phenomenon. That is, only hypotheses that can be *tested* are valid. Often this means that we can control the variables in a system to an extent that allows us to truly determine their effects. If we don't have full control over the variables, for instance, in environmental biology, we can study several different naturally occurring systems in which the desired variable is different.

The scientific method is particularly useful for determining 'cause and effect' type relationships. Thus, appropriate hypotheses are often of this nature. The hypothesis is simply a prediction about a certain behavior that occurs in a system. Then variables are changed to determine whether the hypothesis is correct. For instance, let's consider several identical potted African violets and suppose we have lights of different color, fertilizer, water and a variety of common household items. Below are some possible questions, phrased as hypotheses, and a bit about why they are or are not valid.

1. African violets will grow taller in blue light than they will in red light.
   This hypothesis is valid because it could easily be tested by growing one violet in blue light and another in red. The results are easily observed by measuring the height of the violets.

2. Invisible microbes cause the leaves of African violets to turn yellow.
   This hypothesis is not valid because we cannot know whether a given violet is infected with the microbe. This hypothesis could be tested if we had appropriate technology to detect the presence of the microbe.

3. Lack of water will stop the growth of African violets.
   This hypothesis is also valid because it could be tested by denying water to one violet while continuing to water another. The hypothesis may need to be refined to more specifically define how growth will be measured, but presumably this could be easily done.

4. African violets will not grow well in swamps.
   This hypothesis is not valid in our specific situation because we have only potted plants. It could be tested by actually attempting to grow African violets in a swamp, but that is not within this scenario.

Skill 3.2 Identify processes by which new scientific knowledge and hypotheses are generated

Science may be defined as a body of knowledge that is systematically derived from study, observations, and experimentation. Its goal is to identify and establish principles and theories that may be applied to solve problems. Pseudoscience, on the other hand, is a belief that is not warranted. There is no scientific methodology or application. Some of the more classic examples of pseudoscience include witchcraft, alien encounters or any topic that is explained by hearsay.

Scientific theory and experimentation must be repeatable. It is also possible to be disproved and is capable of change. Science depends on communication, agreement, and disagreement among scientists. It is composed of theories, laws, and hypotheses.

theory - the formation of principles or relationships which have been verified and accepted.

law - an explanation of events that occur with uniformity under the same conditions (laws of nature, law of gravitation).

hypothesis - an unproved theory or educated guess followed by research to best explain a phenomena. A theory is a proven hypothesis.

Science is limited by the available technology. An example of this would be the relationship of the discovery of the cell and the invention of the microscope. As our technology improves, more hypotheses will become theories and possibly laws. Science is also limited by the data that is able to be collected. Data may be interpreted differently on different occasions. Science limitations cause explanations to be changeable as new technologies emerge.

The first step in scientific inquiry is posing a question to be answered. Next, a hypothesis is formed to provide a plausible explanation. An experiment is then proposed and performed to test this hypothesis. A comparison between the predicted and observed results is the next step. Conclusions are then formed and it is determined whether the hypothesis is correct or incorrect. If incorrect, the next step is to form a new hypothesis and the process is repeated.

Skill 3.3 Evaluate the appropriateness of a given experimental design to test a hypothesis

An experiment is proposed and performed with the sole objective of testing a hypothesis. When evaluating an experiment, it is important to first look at the question it was supposed to answer. How logically did the experiment flow from there? How many variables existed (it is best to only test one variable at a time)?

You discover a scientist conducting an experiment with the following characteristics. He has two rows each set up with four stations. The first row has a piece of tile as the base at each station. The second row has a piece of linoleum as the base at each station. The scientist has eight eggs and is prepared to drop one over each station. What is he testing? He is trying to answer whether or not the egg is more likely to break when dropped over one material as opposed to the other. His hypothesis might have been: The egg will be less likely to break when dropped on linoleum. This is a simple experiment. If the experiment was more complicated, or for example, conducted on a microscopic level, one might want to examine the appropriateness of the instruments utilized and their calibration.

Properly collecting data yields information that appropriately answers the original question. For example, one wouldn't try use a graduated cylinder to measure mass, nor would one use a ruler to measure a microscopic item. Utilizing appropriate measuring devices, using proper units and careful mathematics will provide strong results. Carefully evaluating and analyzing the data creates a reasonable conclusion. The conclusion needs to be backed up by scientific criteria, then, finally, communicated to the audience.

Skill 3.4   Analyze ethical issues related to the process of scientific inquiry

Scientists are expected to show good conduct in their scientific pursuits. Conduct here refers to all aspects of scientific activity including experimentation, testing, education, data evaluation, data analysis, data storing, peer review, government funding, the staff, etc.

The following are some of the guiding principles of scientific ethics:

1. Scientific Honesty: not to fraud, fabricate or misinterpret data for personal gain
2. Caution: to avoid errors and sloppiness in all scientific experimentation
3. Credit: give credit where credit is due and not to copy
4. Responsibility: only to report reliable information to public and not to mislead in the name of science
5. Freedom: freedom to criticize old ideas, question new research and freedom to research

Though these principles seem straightforward and clear, it is very difficult to put them into practice because they could be interpreted in more ways than one. Nevertheless, it is not an excuse for scientists to overlook scientific ethics.

To discuss scientific ethics, we can look at natural phenomena like rain. Rain in the normal sense is extremely useful to us and it is absolutely important that there is a water cycle. When rain gets polluted with acid, it becomes acid rain. Here lies the ethical issue of releasing all these pollutants into the atmosphere. Should the scientists communicate the whole truth about acid rain or withhold some information because it may alarm the public? There are many issues like this. Whatever the focus, scientists are expected to be honest and forthright with the public.

TEACHER CERTIFICATION STUDY GUIDE

COMPETENCY 4.0   UNDERSTAND PRINCIPLES OF MEASUREMENT AND THE PROCESSES OF GATHERING, ORGANIZING, REPORTING, AND INTERPRETING SCIENTIFIC DATA

Skill 4.1   Identify procedures for gathering and collecting relevant and reliable data in a given situation

Measurements may be taken in different ways. There is an appropriate measuring device for each aspect of biology. A graduated cylinder is used to measure volume. A balance is used to measure mass. A microscope is used to view microscopic objects. A centrifuge is used to separate two or more parts in a liquid sample. The list goes on, but you get the point. For each variable, there is an appropriate way to measure it. The internet and teaching guides are virtually unlimited resources for laboratory ideas. You should be imparting on the students the importance of the method with which they conduct the study, the resource they use to do so, the concept of double checking their work, and the use of appropriate units.

Skill 4.2   Analyze procedures and formats used in organizing, interpreting, and reporting data (e.g., tables, simple descriptive statistics, graphs)

The type of graphic representation used to display observations depends on the data that is collected. **Line graphs** are used to compare different sets of related data or to predict data that has not yet be measured. An example of a line graph would be comparing the rate of activity of different enzymes at varying temperatures. A **bar graph** or **histogram** is used to compare different items and make comparisons based on this data. An example of a bar graph would be comparing the ages of children in a classroom. A **pie chart** is useful when organizing data as part of a whole. A good use for a pie chart would be displaying the percent of time students spend on various after school activities.

Simple descriptive statistics are meant to describe features of data in a study. This is a description of what was observed or what the data shows. It is not meant to infer anything further, nor does it speculate about what may be. Descriptive Statistics are used to present quantitative descriptions in a manageable form. Consider the infamous the Grade Point Average (GPA). The single number assigned describes a large number of grades, one per each class ever taken. The GPA describes the general performance of the student. While condensing large amounts of information, the danger in descriptive statistics is that the whole picture can become less clear. For example, we don't know if the student had a high GPA because s/he took relatively easy courses, or if the student never took a biology class in their whole collegiate career. There is potentially a wider range of experiences than is encompassed in a descriptive statistic. One should keep this in mind when evaluating a situation or material when only a simple descriptive statistic is provided.

Skill 4.3 Solve problems involving measurements and units of measure

Science uses the **metric system**; as it is accepted worldwide and allows easier comparison among experiments done by scientists around the world.

The meter is the basic metric unit of length. One meter is 1.1 yards. The liter is the basic metric unit of volume. 1 gallon is 3.846 liters. The gram is the basic metric unit of mass. 1000 grams is 2.2 pounds.

The following prefixes are used to describe the multiples of the basic metric units.

deca- 10X the base unit
hecto- 100X the base unit
kilo- 1,000X the base unit
mega- 1,000,000X the base unit
giga- 1,000,000,000X the base unit
tera- 1,000,000,000,000X the base unit

deci - 1/10 the base unit
centi - 1/100 the base unit
milli - 1/1,000 the base unit
micro- 1/1,000,000 the base unit
nano- 1/1,000,000,000 the base unit
pico- 1/1,000,000,000,000 the base unit

TEACHER CERTIFICATION STUDY GUIDE

COMPETENCY 5.0   **UNDERSTAND THE USE OF EQUIPMENT, MATERIALS, AND CHEMICALS IN SCIENTIFIC INQUIRY; AND APPLY PROCEDURES FOR THEIR PROPER, SAFE, AND LEGAL USE**

Skill 5.1   **Apply procedures for selecting and safely using common laboratory equipment (e.g., balances, glassware, thermometers, microscopes)**

Light microscopes are commonly used in high school laboratory experiments. Total magnification is determined by multiplying the ocular (usually 10X) and the objective (usually 10X on low, 40X on high) lenses. Several procedures should be followed to properly care for this equipment.

- Clean all lenses with lens paper only.
- Carry microscopes with two hands; one on the arm and one on the base.
- Always begin focusing on low power, then switch to high power.
- Store microscopes with the low power objective down.
- Always use a coverslip when viewing wet mount slides.
- Bring the objective down to its lowest position then focus moving up to avoid breaking the slide or scratching the lens.

Wet mount slides should be made by placing a drop of water on the specimen and then putting a glass coverslip on top of the drop of water. Dropping the coverslip at a forty-five degree angle will help in avoiding air bubbles.

Chromatography uses the principles of capillarity to separate substances such as plant pigments. Molecules of a larger size will move slower up the paper, whereas smaller molecules will move more quickly producing lines of pigment.

An **indicator** is any substance used to assist in the classification of another substance. An example of an indicator is litmus paper. Litmus paper is a way to measure whether a substance is acidic or basic. Blue litmus turns pink when an acid is placed on it and pink litmus turns blue when a base is placed on it. pH paper is a more accurate measure of pH, with the paper turning different colors depending on the pH value.

Spectrophotometry measures percent of light at different wavelengths absorbed and transmitted by a pigment solution.

Centrifugation involves spinning substances at a high speed. The more dense part of a solution will settle to the bottom of the test tube, where the lighter material will stay on top. Centrifugation is used to separate blood into blood cells and plasma, with the heavier blood cells settling to the bottom.

MID. LEVEL SCIENCE   15

Skill 5.2 Identify procedures for the safe storage, use, and disposal of common laboratory chemicals

All laboratory solutions should be prepared as directed in the lab manual. Care should be taken to avoid contamination. All glassware should be rinsed thoroughly with distilled water before using and cleaned well after use. All solutions should be made with distilled water as tap water contains dissolved particles that may affect the results of an experiment. Unused solutions should be disposed of according to local disposal procedures.

The "Right to Know Law" covers science teachers who work with potentially hazardous chemicals. Briefly, the law states that employees must be informed of potentially toxic chemicals. An inventory must be made available if requested. The inventory must contain information about the hazards and properties of the chemicals. This inventory is to be checked against the "Substance List". Training must be provided on the safe handling and interpretation of the Material Safety Data Sheet.

The following chemicals are potential carcinogens and not allowed in school facilities: Acrylonitriel, Arsenic compounds, Asbestos, Bensidine, Benzene, Cadmium compounds, Chloroform, Chromium compounds, Ethylene oxide, Ortho-toluidine, Nickle powder, and Mercury.

Chemicals should not be stored on bench tops or heat sources. They should be stored in groups based on their reactivity with one another and in protective storage cabinets. All containers within the lab must be labeled. Suspect and known carcinogens must be labeled as such and segregated within trays to contain leaks and spills.

Chemical waste should be disposed of in properly labeled containers. Waste should be separated based on their reactivity with other chemicals.

Biological material should never be stored near food or water used for human consumption. All biological material should be appropriately labeled. All blood and body fluids should be put in a well-contained container with a secure lid to prevent leaking. All biological waste should be disposed of in biological hazardous waste bags.

Material safety data sheets are available for every chemical and biological substance. These are available directly from the company of acquisition or the internet. The manuals for equipment used in the lab should be read and understood before using them.

Skill 5.3 **Identify procedures for the proper and humane treatment and safe handling of classroom animals**

No dissections may be performed on living mammalian vertebrates or birds. Lower order life and invertebrates may be used. Biological experiments may be done with all animals except mammalian vertebrates or birds. No physiological harm may result to the animal. All animals housed and cared for in the school must be handled in a safe and humane manner. Animals are not to remain on school premises during extended vacations unless adequate care is provided. Any instructor who intentionally refuses to comply with the laws may be suspended or dismissed.

Pathogenic organisms must never be used for experimentation. Students should adhere to the following rules at all times when working with microorganisms to avoid accidental contamination:

1. Treat all microorganisms as if they were pathogenic.
2. Maintain sterile conditions at all times

Skill 5.4 **Apply procedures for promoting laboratory safety and appropriately responding to accidents and injuries in the science laboratory**

All science labs should contain the following items of **safety equipment**. Those marked with an asterisk are requirements by state laws.

* fire blanket which is visible and accessible
*Ground Fault Circuit Interrupters (GCFI) within two feet of water supplies
*signs designating room exits
*emergency shower providing a continuous flow of water
*emergency eye wash station which can be activated by the foot or forearm
*eye protection for every student and a means of sanitizing equipment
*emergency exhaust fans providing ventilation to the outside of the building
*master cut-off switches for gas, electric and compressed air. Switches must have permanently attached handles. Cut-off switches must be clearly labeled.
*an ABC fire extinguisher
*storage cabinets for flammable materials
-chemical spill control kit
-fume hood with a motor which is spark proof
-protective laboratory aprons made of flame retardant material
-signs which will alert potential hazardous conditions
-containers for broken glassware, flammables, corrosives, and waste
-Containers should be labeled.

Students should wear safety goggles when performing dissections, heating, or while using acids and bases. Hair should always be tied back and objects should never be placed in the mouth. Food should not be consumed while in the laboratory. Hands should always be washed before and after laboratory experiments. In case of an accident, eye washes and showers should be used for eye contamination or a chemical spill that covers the student's body. Small chemical spills should only be contained and cleaned by the teacher. Kitty litter or a chemical spill kit should be used to clean spill. For large spills, the school administration and the local fire department should be notified. Biological spills should also be handled only by the teacher. Contamination with biological waste can be cleaned by using bleach when appropriate.
Accidents and injuries should always be reported to the school administration and local health facilities. The severity of the accident or injury will determine the course of action to pursue.

It is the responsibility of the teacher to provide a safe environment for their students. Proper supervision greatly reduces the risk of injury and a teacher should never leave a class for any reason without providing alternate supervision. After an accident, two factors are considered; **foreseeability** and **negligence**. Foreseeability is the anticipation that an event may occur under certain circumstances. Negligence is the failure to exercise ordinary or reasonable care. Safety procedures should be a part of the science curriculum and a well-managed classroom is important to avoid potential lawsuits.

SUBAREA II.   **LIFE SCIENCE**

COMPETENCY 6.0   UNDERSTAND BASIC CONCEPTS OF CELL BIOLOGY

Skill 6.1   **Identify the components and principles of the cell theory**

Cell theory states that all living organisms are made up of cells that are essentially the same chemically, are the fundamental unit of life, and arise from preexisting cells through cell division. Advances in microscopic technology initiated the development of cell theory.

The invention of the microscope in the 17th century allowed scientists to observe microscopic life and begin to identify microscopic structures. Athanasius Kircher and Antoni van Leeuwenhoek first observed maggots in decaying tissue and microorganisms (protozoa and other unicellular organisms) respectively. In 1665, Robert Hooke provided the first description of the cell. Hooke labeled the microscopic units that made up a slice of cork as "cells".

Experiments by Lazzaro Spallanzani and Louis Pasteur in the 18th and 19th centuries clarified the distinction between living and non-living matter. Spallanzani and Pasteur showed that living organisms derive from other living organisms, thus disproving the theory of spontaneous generation, or life from non-life.

In 1838, botanist Matthias Schleiden theorized that cells and cellular products constitute all structural elements of plants. A year later zoologist Theodor Schwann reached the same conclusion about the structural elements of animals. The findings of Schleiden and Schwann represent the initial formulation of cell theory.

Cell theory continued to develop in the late 19th century with the identification of protoplasmic organelles. Finally, Walther Flemming observed the components of the nucleus and nucleolus. Through staining, Flemming observed chromosomes during cell division and first coined the term mitosis.

Skill 6.2   Recognize basic cell structures and their functions

Parts of Eukaryotic Cells

1. Nucleus - The brain of the cell. The nucleus contains:
   chromosomes- DNA, RNA and proteins tightly coiled to conserve space while providing a large surface area.
   chromatin - loose structure of chromosomes. Chromosomes are called chromatin when the cell is not dividing.
   nucleoli - where ribosomes are made. These are seen as dark spots in the nucleus.
   nuclear membrane - contains pores which let RNA out of the nucleus. The nuclear membrane is continuous with the endoplasmic reticulum which allows the membrane to expand or shrink if needed.

2. Ribosomes - the site of protein synthesis. Ribosomes may be free floating in the cytoplasm or attached to the endoplasmic reticulum. There may be up to a half a million ribosomes in a cell, depending on how much protein is made by the cell.

3. Endoplasmic Reticulum - These are folded and provide a large surface area. They are the "roadway" of the cell and allow for transport of materials throughout and out of the cell. The lumen of the endoplasmic reticulum helps to keep materials out of the cytoplasm and headed in the right direction. The endoplasmic reticulum is capable of building new membrane material. There are two types:

   Smooth Endoplasmic Reticulum - contain no ribosomes on their surface.
   Rough Endoplasmic Reticulum - contain ribosomes on their surface. This form of ER is abundant in cells that make many proteins, like in the pancreas, which produces many digestive enzymes.

4. Golgi Complex or Golgi Apparatus - This is a stacked structure to increase surface area. The Golgi Complex functions to sort, modify and package molecules that are made in other parts of the cells. These molecules are either sent out of the cell or to other organelles within the cell.

5. Lysosomes - found mainly in animal cells. These contain digestive enzymes that break down food, substances not needed, viruses, damaged cell components and eventually the cell itself. It is believed that lysosomes are responsible for the aging process.

6. Mitochondria - large organelles that make ATP to supply energy to the cell. Muscle cells have many mitochondria because they use a great deal of energy. The folds inside the mitochondria are called cristae. They provide a large surface area for the reactions of cellular respiration to occur. Mitochondria have their own DNA and are capable of reproducing themselves if a greater demand is made for additional energy. Mitochondria are found only in animal cells.

7. Vacuoles - hold stored food and pigments. Vacuoles are very large in plants. This is allows them to fill with water in order to provide turgor pressure. Lack of turgor pressure causes a plant to wilt.

8. Cytoskeleton - composed of protein filaments attached to the plasma membrane and organelles. They provide a framework for the cell and aid in cell movement. They constantly change shape and move about. Three types of fibers make up the cytoskeleton: microtubules, intermediate filaments, and microfilaments.

    Microtubules - largest of the three makes up cilia and flagella for locomotion. Flagella grow from a basal body. Some examples are sperm cells, and tracheal cilia. Centrioles are also composed of microtubules. They form the spindle fibers that pull the cell apart into two cells during cell division. Centrioles are not found in the cells of higher plants. Intermediate Filaments - they are smaller than microtubules but larger than microfilaments. They help the cell to keep its shape. Microfilaments - smallest of the three, they are made of actin and small amounts of myosin (like in muscle cells). They function in cell movement like cytoplasmic streaming, endocytosis and ameboid movement.
    This structure pinches the two cells apart after cell division, forming two cells.

Skill 6.3 **Compare the structure of animal and plant cells**

Plant cells are organized differently from animal cells. Found only in plant cells, the **cell wall** is composed of cellulose and fibers. It is thick enough for support and protection, yet porous enough to allow water and dissolved substances to enter. **Vacuoles** are found mostly in plant cells. They hold stored food and pigments. Their large size allows them to fill with water in order to provide turgor pressure. Lack of turgor pressure causes a plant to wilt. Cytoskeletons are found in both plants and animals. They are composed of protein filaments attached to the plasma membrane and organelles. They provide a framework for the cell and aid in cell movement. They constantly change shape and move about. Three types of fibers make up the cytoskeleton: microtubules, intermediate filaments, and microfilaments. Centrioles, a kind of microtubule, are found in animals but not in higher plants. Plastids are found in photosynthetic organisms only. They are similar to an animal's mitochondria due to their double membrane structure. They also have their own DNA and can reproduce if the need for the increased capture of sunlight becomes necessary. There are several types of plastids:

> Chloroplasts - green, function in photosynthesis. They are capable of trapping sunlight.
> Chromoplasts - make and store yellow and orange pigments; they provide color to leaves, flowers and fruits.
> Amyloplasts - store starch and are used as a food reserve. They are abundant in roots like potatoes.

Skill 6.4   **Identify the role of organic molecules (e.g., proteins, DNA, carbohydrates) in cells and organisms**

A compound consists of two or more elements. There are four major chemical compounds found in the cells and bodies of living things. These include carbohydrates, lipids, proteins and nucleic acids.

Monomers are the simplest unit of structure. **Monomers** can be combined to form **polymers**, or long chains, making a large variety of molecules possible. Monomers combine through the process of condensation reaction (also called dehydration synthesis). In this process, one molecule of water is removed between each of the adjoining molecules. In order to break the molecules apart in a polymer, water molecules are added between monomers, thus breaking the bonds between them. This is called hydrolysis.

Carbohydrates contain a ratio of two hydrogen atoms for each carbon and oxygen $(CH_2O)_n$. Carbohydrates include sugars and starches. They function in the release of energy. **Monosaccharides** are the simplest sugars and include glucose, fructose, and galactose. They are major nutrients for cells. In cellular respiration, the cells extract the energy in glucose molecules. **Disaccharides** are made by joining two monosaccharides by condensation to form a glycosidic linkage (covalent bond between two monosaccharides). Maltose is formed from the combination of two glucose molecules, lactose is formed from joining glucose and galactose, and sucrose is formed from the combination of glucose and fructose. **Polysaccharides** consist of many monomers joined. They are storage material hydrolyzed as needed to provide sugar for cells or building material for structures protecting the cell. Examples of polysaccharides include starch, glycogen, cellulose and chitin.

> **Starch** - major energy storage molecule in plants. It is a polymer consisting of glucose monomers.
> **Glycogen** - major energy storage molecule in animals. It is made up of many glucose molecules.
> **Cellulose** - found in plant cell walls, its function is structural. Many animals lack the enzymes necessary to hydrolyze cellulose, so it simply adds bulk (fiber) to the diet.
> **Chitin** - found in the exoskeleton of arthropods and fungi. Chitin contains an amino sugar (glycoprotein).

Lipids are composed of glycerol (an alcohol) and three fatty acids. Lipids are **hydrophobic** (water fearing) and will not mix with water. There are three important families of lipids, fats, phospholipids and steroids. **Fats** consist of glycerol (alcohol) and three fatty acids. Fatty acids are long carbon skeletons. The nonpolar carbon-hydrogen bonds in the tails of fatty acids are why they are hydrophobic. Fats are solids at room temperature and come from animal sources (butter, lard). **Phospholipids** are a vital component in cell membranes. In a phospholipid, one or two fatty acids are replaced by a phosphate group linked to a nitrogen group. They consist of a **polar** (charged) head that is hydrophilic or water loving and a **nonpolar** (uncharged) tail which is hydrophobic or water fearing. This allows the membrane to orient itself with the polar heads facing the interstitial fluid found outside the cell and the internal fluid of the cell.

Proteins compose about fifty percent of the dry weight of animals and bacteria. Proteins function in structure and aid in support (connective tissue, hair, feathers, quills), storage of amino acids (albumin in eggs, casein in milk), transport of substances (hemoglobin), hormonal to coordinate body activities (insulin), membrane receptor proteins, contraction (muscles, cilia, flagella), body defense (antibodies), and as enzymes to speed up chemical reactions. All proteins are made of twenty **amino acids**. An amino acid contains an amino group and an acid group. The radical group varies and defines the amino acid. Amino acids form through condensation reactions with the removal of water. The bond that is formed between two amino acids is called a peptide bond. Polymers of amino acids are called polypeptide chains. An analogy can be drawn between the twenty amino acids and the alphabet. Millions of words can be formed using an alphabet of only twenty-six letters. This diversity is also possible using only twenty amino acids. This results in the formation of many different proteins, whose structure defines the function. There are four levels of protein structure: primary, secondary, tertiary, and quaternary.

Nucleic acids consist of DNA (deoxyribonucleic acid) and RNA (ribonucleic acid). Nucleic acids contain the instructions for the amino acid sequence of proteins and the instructions for replicating. The monomer of nucleic acids is called a nucleotide. A nucleotide consists of a 5 carbon sugar, (deoxyribose in DNA, ribose in RNA), a phosphate group, and a nitrogenous base. The base sequence codes for the instructions. There are five bases: adenine, thymine, cytosine, guanine, and uracil. Uracil is found only in RNA and replaces the thymine.

COMPETENCY 7.0 UNDERSTAND CHARACTERISTICS OF LIFE AND BASIC LIFE PROCESS

Skill 7.1 Recognize differences between organisms and nonliving things

Several characteristics have been described to identify living versus non-living substances.
1. Living things are made of cells; they grow, are capable of reproduction and respond to stimuli.
2. Living things must adapt to environmental changes or perish.
3. Living things carry on metabolic processes. They use and make energy.

Skill 7.2 Identify the characteristics of major groups of organisms

Nonvascular Plants - small in size, did not require vascular tissue (xylem and phloem) as individual cells were close to their environment. The nonvascular plants have no true leaves, stems or roots. Division Bryophyta - mosses and liverworts, these plants have a dominant gametophyte generation. They possess rhizoids, which are root like structures. Moisture in their environment is required for reproduction and absorption.

Vascular Plants - the development of vascular tissue enabled these plants to grow in size. Xylem and phloem allowed for the transport of water and minerals up to the top of the plant and food manufactured in the leaves to the bottom of the plant. All vascular plants have a dominant sporophyte generation.

Division Lycophyta - club mosses; these plants reproduce with spores and require water for reproduction.

Division Sphenophyta - horsetails; also reproduce with spores. These plants have small, needle-like leaves and rhizoids. Require moisture for reproduction.

Division Pterophyta - ferns; reproduce with spores and flagellated sperm. These plants have true stem and need moisture for reproduction.

Gymnosperms - The word means "naked seed". These were the first plants to evolve with the use of seeds for reproduction which made them less dependent on water to assist in reproduction. Their seeds could travel by wind. Pollen from the male was also easily carried by the wind. Gymnosperms have cones that protect the seeds.

Division Cycadophyta - cycads; these plants look like palms with cones.

Davison Ghetophyta - desert dwellers.

Division Coniferophyta - pines; these plants have needles and cones.

Division Ginkgophyta - the Ginkgo is the only member of this division.

Angiosperms (Division Anthophyta) - Angiosperms are the largest group in the plant kingdom. They are the flowering plants and produce true seeds for reproduction.

Annelida - the segmented worms; the first with specialized tissue. The circulatory system is more advanced in these worms and is a closed system with blood vessels. The nephridia are their excretory organs. They are hermaphrodidic and each worm fertilizes the other upon mating. They support themselves with a hydrostatic skeleton and have circular and longitudinal muscles for movement.

Mollusca - clams, octopus; the soft bodied animals. These animals have a muscular foot for movement. They breathe through gills and most are able to make a shell for protection from predators. They have an open circulatory system, with sinuses bathing the body regions.

Arthropoda - insects, crustaceans and spiders; this is the largest group of the animal kingdom. Phylum arthropoda accounts for about 85% of all the animal species. Animals in the arthropoda phylum possess an exoskeleton made of chitin. They must molt to grow. Insects, for example, go through four stages of development. They begin as an egg, hatches into a larva, forms a pupa, then emerges as an adult. Arthropods breathe through gills, trachae or book lungs. Movement varies, with members being able to swim, fly and crawl. There is a division of labor among the appendages (legs, antennae, etc). This is an extremely successful phylum, with members occupying diverse habitats.

Echinodermata - sea urchins and starfish; these animals have spiny skin. Their habitat is marine. They have tube feet for locomotion and feeding.

Chordata - all animals with a notocord or a backbone. The classes in this phylum include:
Agnatha (jawless fish)
Chondrichthyes (cartilage fish)
Osteichthyes (bony fish)
Amphibia (frogs and toads; gills are replaced by lungs during development)
Reptilia (snakes, lizards; the first to lay eggs with a protective covering)
Aves (birds; warm-blooded with wings consisting of a particular shape and composition designed for flight)
Mammalia (animals with body hair that bear their young alive, possess mammary glands that produce milk, and are warm-blooded).

Skill 7.3   **Analyze the processes of photosynthesis and cellular respiration**

Photosynthesis is the process by which plants make carbohydrates from the energy of the sun, carbon dioxide and water. Oxygen is a waste product. Photosynthesis occurs in the chloroplast where the pigment chlorophyll traps sun energy. It is divided into two major steps:

> **Light Reactions** - Sunlight is trapped, water is split, and oxygen is given off. ATP is made and hydrogens reduce NADP to NADPH2. The light reactions occur in light. The products of the light reactions enter into the dark reactions (Calvin cycle).

> **Dark Reactions** - Carbon dioxide enters during the dark reactions which can occur with or without the presence of light. The energy transferred from NADPH2 and ATP allow for the fixation of carbon into glucose.

Cellular respiration is the metabolic pathway in which food (glucose, etc.) is broken down to produce energy in the form of ATP. Both plants and animals utilize respiration to create energy for metabolism. In respiration, energy is released by the transfer of electrons in a process know as an **oxidation-reduction (redox)** reaction. During times of decreased light, plants break down the products of photosynthesis through cellular respiration. Glucose, with the help of oxygen breaks down and produces carbon dioxide and water as wastes. Approximately fifty percent of the products of photosynthesis are used by the plant for energy. Below is a diagram of the relationship between cellular respiration and photosynthesis.

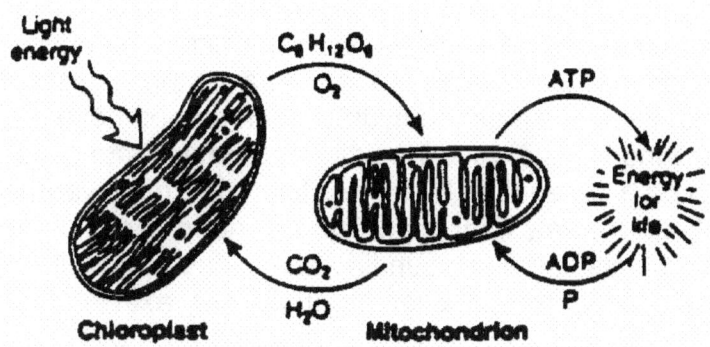

Skill 7.4 Analyze basic life processes (e.g., homeostasis, reproduction, growth)

Homeostasis

All living organisms respond and adapt to their environments. Homeostasis is the result of regulatory mechanisms that help maintain an organism's internal environment within tolerable limits. It is important to recognize that homeostasis is not an independent process in and of itself. Instead, homeostasis is the combined result of many smaller changes throughout multiple parts of an organism. These small changes and cycles result in the overall state of constancy, which ensures survival. For example, cell transport allows a cell to be balanced with its external environment. Cell membranes are selectively permeable, which is the key to transport. Not all molecules may pass through easily. In humans and mammals, the skeletal system acts as a buffer in maintaining calcium homeostasis by absorbing or releasing calcium as needed. The muscular system contributes to homeostasis in two ways. First, muscle contraction produces heat as a by-product. This heat helps maintain the body's internal temperature. Second, the muscular system (in coordination with the skeletal system) allows organisms to move to environments that are more favorable from a homeostatic perspective. The circulatory system plays a vital role in homeostasis. The circulatory system delivers nutrients and removes waste from all the body's tissue by pumping blood through blood vessels. Constriction and dilation of blood vessels near the skin help maintain body temperature. The entire function of the immune system is homeostatic in nature. The immune system protects the body's internal environment from invading microorganisms, viruses, and cancerous cells.

Reproduction

Reproduction may occur via sexual or asexual methods. The obvious advantage of asexual reproduction is that it does not require a partner. This is a huge advantage for organisms, such as the hydra, which do not move around. Not having to move around to reproduce also allows organisms to conserve energy. Asexual reproduction also tends to be faster. There are disadvantages, as in the case of regeneration, in plants if the plant is not in good condition or in the case of spore-producing plants, if the surrounding conditions are not suitable for the spores to grow. As asexual reproduction produces only exact copies of the parent organism, it does not allow for genetic variation, which means that mutations, or weaker qualities, will always be passed on. This can also be detrimental to a species well-adapted to a particular environment when the conditions of that environment change suddenly. On the whole, asexual reproduction is more reliable because it requires fewer steps and less can go wrong.

Sexual reproduction shares genetic information between gametes, thereby producing variety in the species. This can result in a better species with an improved chance of survival. There is the disadvantage that sexual reproduction requires a partner, which, in turn, with many organisms requires courtship, finding a mate, and mating. Another disadvantage is that sexually reproductive organisms require special mechanisms.

Growth

Individuals grow by increasing their surface area (ie., cellular size and quantity). In higher animals, cellular differentiation occurs when certain genes are activated and others are inactivated. Soluble factors called morphogens are responsible for turning these genes on and off. Well known morphogens include transforming growth factor beta, hedgehog, and epidermal growth factor. Another type of soluble factor, mitogens, are responsible for triggering mitosis that leads to cell division. A variety of substances ranging from antigens to fibroblast growth factor can act as mitogens. Whether cells grow, divide, or differentiate depends upon the local concentration of these various factors. These factors may be present as part of natural development. For example, during embryonic development both morphogens and mitogens are produced to provide ample amounts of the various tissue needed by the organism. Mechanical stimulus may also affect cell growth and differentiation. For instance, increased mechanical loading of bones causes the formation of additional bone and osteocytes. Finally, foreign substances may serve as morphogens or mitogens. Plasma B cells, for example, enter mitosis when they encounter an antigen matching their immunoglobulin.

Skill 7.5   Identify the structure, components, functions, and physiological processes of organs and systems in plants and animals (including humans)

The organization of living systems builds by levels from small to increasingly more large and complex. All aspects, whether it be a cell or an ecosystem, have the same requirements to sustain life. Life is organized from simple to complex in the following way:

Organelles make up **cells,** which make up **tissues,** which make up **organs**. Groups of organs make up **organ systems**. Organ systems work together to provide life for the **organism.**

Skeletal System - The skeletal system functions in support. Vertebrates have an endoskeleton, with muscles attached to bones. Skeletal proportions are controlled by area to volume relationships. Body size and shape is limited due to the forces of gravity. Surface area is increased to improve efficiency in all organ systems.

Muscular System – Its function is for movement. There are three types of muscle tissue. Skeletal muscle is voluntary. These muscles are attached to bones. Smooth muscle is involuntary. It is found in organs and enable functions such as digestion and respiration. Cardiac muscle is a specialized type of smooth muscle.

Nervous System - The neuron is the basic unit of the nervous system. It consists of an axon, which carries impulses away from the cell body, the dendrite, which carries impulses toward the cell body and the cell body, which contains the nucleus. Synapses are spaces between neurons. Chemicals called neurotransmitters are found close to the synapse. The myelin sheath, composed of Schwann cells, covers the neurons and provides insulation.

Digestive System - The function of the digestive system is to break down food and absorb it into the blood stream where it can be delivered to all cells of the body for use in cellular respiration. As animals evolved, digestive systems changed from simple absorption to a system with a separate mouth and anus, capable of allowing the animal to become independent of a host.

Respiratory System - This system functions in the gas exchange of oxygen (needed) and carbon dioxide (waste). It delivers oxygen to the bloodstream and picks up carbon dioxide for release out of the body. Simple animals diffuse gases from and to their environment. Gills allow aquatic animals to exchange gases in a fluid medium by removing dissolved oxygen from the water. Lungs maintain a fluid environment for gas exchange in terrestrial animals.

Circulatory System - The function of the circulatory system is to carry oxygenated blood and nutrients to all cells of the body and return carbon dioxide waste to be expelled from the lungs. Animals evolved from an open system to a closed system with vessels leading to and from the heart.

COMPETENCY 8.0 UNDERSTAND GENETICS AND BIOLOGICAL ADAPTATION

Skill 8.1 Identify the structure and function of genes and chromosomes

Chromosomes are the physical structures found in every cell, which carry the genetic information of an organism and function in the transmission of hereditary information. Each chromosome contains a sequence of genes each with a specific locus. A locus is the position a given gene occupies on a chromosome. Each gene consists of a sequence of DNA that dictates a particular characteristic of an organism. Separating the genes on a chromosome are regions of DNA that do not code for proteins or other cellular products, but may function in the regulation of coding regions.

Skill 8.2 Analyze processes by which characteristics are passed on from parents to offspring

Gregor Mendel is recognized as the father of genetics. His work in the late 1800s is the basis of our knowledge of genetics. Although unaware of the presence of DNA or genes, Mendel realized there were factors (now known as **genes**) that were transferred from parents to their offspring. Mendel worked with pea plants and fertilized the plants himself, keeping track of subsequent generations which led to the Mendelian laws of genetics. Mendel found that two "factors" governed each trait, one from each parent. Traits or characteristics came in several forms, known as **alleles**. For example, the trait of flower color had white alleles (*pp*) and purple alleles (*PP*). Mendel formed two laws: the law of segregation and the law of independent assortment.

The **law of segregation** states that only one of the two possible alleles from each parent is passed on to the offspring. If the two alleles differ, then one is fully expressed in the organism's appearance (the dominant allele) and the other has no noticeable effect on appearance (the recessive allele). The two alleles for each trait segregate into different gametes. A Punnet square can be used to show the law of segregation. In a Punnet square, one parent's genes are put at the top of the box and the other parent's on the side. Genes combine in the squares just like numbers are added in addition tables. This Punnet square shows the result of the cross of two F_1 hybrids.

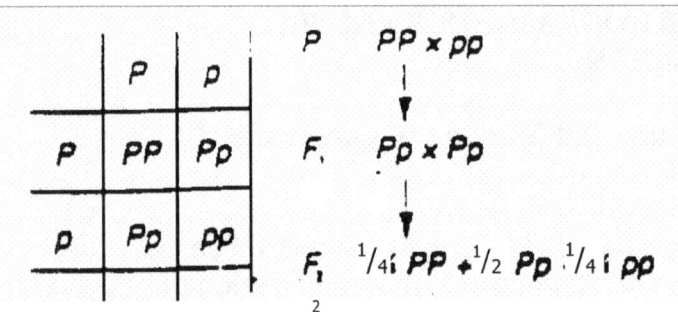

This cross results in a 1:2:1 ratio of F_2 offspring. Here, the *P* is the dominant allele and the *p* is the recessive allele. The F_1 cross produces three offspring with the dominant allele expressed (two *PP* and *Pp*) and one offspring with the recessive allele expressed (*pp*). Some other important terms to know:

> **Homozygous** – having a pair of identical alleles. For example, *PP* and *pp* are homozygous pairs.
> **Heterozygous** – having two different alleles. For example, *Pp* is a heterozygous pair.
> **Phenotype** – the organism's physical appearance.
> **Genotype** – the organism's genetic makeup. For example, *PP* and *Pp* have the same phenotype (purple in color), but different genotypes.

The **law of independent assortment** states that alleles sort independently of each other. The law of segregation applies for a monohybrid crosses (only one character, in this case flower color, is experimented with). In a dihybrid cross, two characters are being explored. Two of the seven characters Mendel studied were seed shape and color. Yellow is the dominant seed color (*Y*) and green is the recessive color (*y*). The dominant seed shape is round (*R*) and the recessive shape is wrinkled (*r*). A cross between a plant with yellow round seeds (*YYRR*) and a plant with green wrinkled seeds (*yyrr*) produces an F_1 generation with the genotype *YyRr*. The production of F_2 offspring results in a 9:3:3:1 phenotypic ratio.

	YR	Yr	yR	yr
YR	YYRR	YYRr	YyRR	YyRr
Yr	YYRr	YYrr	YyRr	Yyrr
yR	YyRR	YyRr	yyRR	yyRr
yr	YyRr	Yyrr	yyRr	yyrr

P   YYRR × yyrr
          ↓
F_1 YyRr
          ↓
F_2 YYRR – 1
    YYRr – 2 } 9 yellow round
    YyRR – 2
    YyRr – 4

    yyRR – 1 } 3 green round
    yyRr – 2

    YYrr – 1 } 3 yellow wrinkled
    Yyrr – 2

    yyrr – 1 } 1 green wrinkled

Based on Mendelian genetics, the more complex hereditary pattern of **dominance** was discovered. In Mendel's law of segregation, the F_1 generation has either purple or white flowers. This is an example of **complete dominance**. **Incomplete dominance** is when the F_1 generation results in an appearance somewhere between the two parents. For example, red flowers are crossed with white flowers, resulting in an F_1 generation with pink flowers. The red and white traits are still carried by the F_1 generation, resulting in an F_2 generation with a phenotypic ration of 1:2:1. In **codominance,** the genes may form new phenotypes. The ABO blood grouping is an example of codominance. A and B are of equal strength and O is recessive. Therefore, type A blood may have the genotypes of AA or AO, type B blood may have the genotypes of BB or BO, type AB blood has the genotype A and B, and type O blood has two recessive O genes.

Skill 8.3 Analyze the roles of variation, natural selection, and adaptation in biological evolution

Variations occur naturally within a population. Some of these variations will aid an individual, others will harm, and still others will have no effect on one's survival. Those individuals with positive variations will best survive and produce offspring that are more adapted to the environment. The colorations of plants and animals serve as camouflage or as warning in their environments. Cryptic coloration is that color or pattern that serves to conceal. For example, moths with light-colored wings are nearly invisible on birch trees (their chosen home), but are obvious to all birds, and therefore eaten, when they land on a dark tree trunk. In grasshoppers, only green ones are seen in areas where there is abundant lush grass but only tan and brown ones are seen in dry prairie areas. Those that do not match their environment do not survive to reproduce. Most animals (including many birds and insects) are darker on their backs than underneath. This tends to conceal them since most light comes from above and is absorbed by the darkness of their upper bodies.

Natural selection is based on the survival of certain traits in a population through the course of time. The phrase "survival of the fittest," is often associated with natural selection. Fitness is the contribution an individual makes to the gene pool of the next generation.

Natural selection acts on phenotypes. An organism's phenotype is constantly exposed to its environment. Based on an organism's phenotype, selection indirectly adapts a population to its environment by maintaining favorable genotypes in the gene pool.

There are three modes of natural selection. Stabilizing selection favors the more common phenotypes, directional selection shifts the frequency of phenotypes in one direction, and diversifying selection occurs when individuals on both extremes of the phenotypic range are favored.

Sexual selection leads to the secondary sex characteristics between male and females. Animals that use mating behaviors may be successful or unsuccessful. An animal that lacks attractive plumage or has a weak mating call will not attract the female, thereby eventually limiting that gene in the gene pool. Mechanical isolation, where sex organs do not fit the female, has an obvious disadvantage.

Anatomical structures and physiological processes that evolve over geological time to increase the overall reproductive success of an organism in its environment are known **as biological adaptations**. Such evolutionary changes occur through natural selection, the process by which individual organisms with favorable traits survive to reproduce more frequently than those with unfavorable traits. The heritable component of such favorable traits is passed down to offspring during reproduction, increasing the frequency of the favorable trait in a population over many generations.

Adaptations increase long-term reproductive success by making an organism better suited for survival under particular environmental conditions and pressures. These biological changes can increase an organism's ability to obtain air, water, food and nutrients, to cope with environmental variables and to defend themselves. The term adaptation may apply to changes in biological processes that, for example, enable an organism to produce venom or to regulate body temperature, and also to structural adaptations, such as an organism's skin color and shape. Adaptations can occur in behavioral traits and survival mechanisms as well.

COMPETENCY 9.0 UNDERSTAND POPULATIONS, COMMUNITIES, ECOSYSTEMS, AND BIOMES

Skill 9.1 Identify the characteristics of populations, communities, ecosystems, and biomes

Ecology is the study of organisms, where they live and their interactions with the environment. A population is a group of the same species in a specific area. A community is a group of populations residing in the same area. Communities that are ecologically similar in regards to temperature, rainfall and the species that live there are called biomes. Specific biomes include:

Marine - covers 75% of the earth. This biome is organized by the depth of the water. The intertidal zone is from the tide line to the edge of the water. The littoral zone is from the waters' edge to the open sea. It includes coral reef habitats and is the most densely populated area of the marine biome. The open sea zone is divided into the epipelagic zone and the pelagic zone. The epipelagic zone receives more sunlight and has a larger number of species. The ocean floor is called the benthic zone and is populated with bottom feeders.

Tropical Rain Forest - temperature is constant (25 degrees C), rainfall exceeds 200 cm. per year. Located around the area of the equator, the rain forest has abundant, diverse species of plants and animals.

Savanna - temperatures range from 0 - 25 degrees C depending on the location. Rainfall is from 90 to 150 cm per year. Plants include shrubs and grasses. The savanna is a transitional biome between the rain forest and the desert.

Desert - temperatures range from 10 - 38 degrees C. Rainfall is under 25 cm per year. Plant species include xerophytes and succulents. Lizards, snakes and small mammals are common animals.

Temperate Deciduous Forest - temperature ranges from -24 to 38 degrees C. Rainfall is between 65 to 150 cm per year. Deciduous trees are common, as well as deer, bear and squirrels.

Taiga - temperatures range from -24 to 22 degrees C. Rainfall is between 35 to 40 cm per year. Taiga is located very north and very south of the equator, getting close to the poles. Plant life includes conifers and plants that can withstand harsh winters. Animals include weasels, mink, and moose.

Tundra - temperatures range from -28 to 15 degrees C. Rainfall is limited, ranging from 10 to 15 cm per year. The tundra is located even further north and south of the taiga. Common plants include lichens and mosses. Animals include polar bears and musk ox.

Polar or Permafrost - temperature ranges from -40 to 0 degrees C. It rarely gets above freezing. Rainfall is below 10 cm per year. Most water is bound up as ice. Life is limited.

Skill 9.2 Analyze factors that affect population growth and community interactions

Definitions of feeding relationships (community interactions):

Parasitism - two species that occupy a similar place; the parasite benefits from the relationship; the host is harmed.
Commensalism - two species that occupy a similar place; neither species is harmed or benefits from the relationship.
Mutualism (symbiosis)- two species that occupy a similar place; both species benefit from the relationship.
Competition - two species that occupy the same habitat or eat the same food are said to be in competition with each other.
Predation - animals that eat other animals are called predators. The animals they feed on are called the prey. Population growth depends upon competition for food, water, shelter and space. The amount of predators determines the amount of prey, which in turn affects the number of predators.

Population growth

A **population** is a group of individuals of one species that live in the same general area. Many factors can affect the population size and its growth rate. Population size can depend on the total amount of life a habitat can support. This is the carrying capacity of the environment. Once the habitat runs out of food, water, shelter, or space, the carrying capacity decreases, and then stabilizes.

Limiting factors can affect population growth. As a population increases, the competition for resources is more intense, and the growth rate declines. This is a **density-dependent** growth factor. The carrying capacity can be determined by the density-dependent factor. **Density-independent factors** affect the individuals regardless of population size. The weather and climate are good examples. Too hot or too cold temperatures may kill many individuals from a population that has not reached its carrying capacity.

Global warming - rainforest depletion and the use of fossil fuels and aerosols have caused an increase in carbon dioxide production. This leads to a decrease in the amount of oxygen, which is directly proportional to the amount of ozone. As the ozone layer depletes, more heat enters our atmosphere and is trapped. This causes an overall warming effect, which may eventually melt polar ice caps, causing a rise in water levels and changes in climate, which will affect weather systems.

Endangered species - construction to house our overpopulated world has caused a destruction of habitat for other animals leading to extinction.

Overpopulation - the human race is still growing at an exponential rate.

Carrying Capacity - this is the total amount of life a habitat can support. Once the habitat runs out of food, water, shelter or space, the carrying capacity decreases, and then stabilizes. Our carrying capacity has not been met due to our ability to use technology to produce more food and housing. Space and water can not be manufactured and eventually our overuse affects every living thing on this planet.

Zero population growth rate occurs when the birth and death rates are equal in a population. Exponential growth rate occurs when there is and abundance of resources and the growth rate is at its maximum, called the intrinsic rate of increase. This relationship can be understood in a growth curve.

An exponentially growing population starts off with a little change, then rapidly increases.

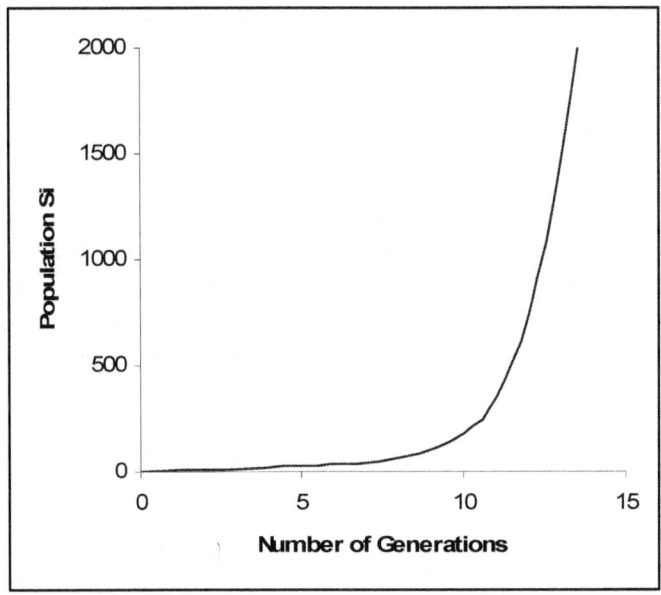

Logistic population growth incorporates the carrying capacity into the growth rate. As a population reaches the carrying capacity, the growth rate begins to slow down and level off.

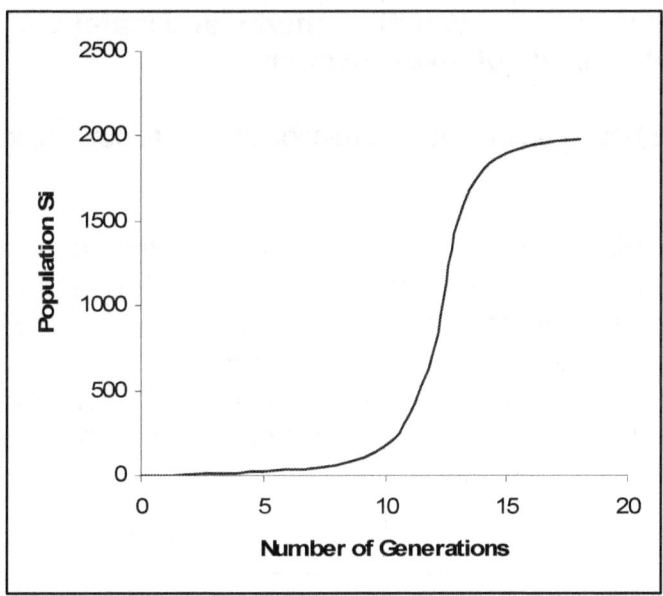

Many populations follow this model of population growth. Humans, however, are an exponentially growing population. Eventually, the carrying capacity of the Earth will be reached, and the growth rate will level off. How and when this will occur remains a mystery.

Skill 9.3 Analyze the movement of energy and materials through the trophic levels of an ecosystem

Trophic levels are based on the feeding relationships that determine energy flow and chemical cycling.

Autotrophs are the primary producers of the ecosystem. **Producers** mainly consist of plants. **Primary consumers** are the next trophic level. The primary consumers are the herbivores that eat plants or algae. **Secondary consumers** are the carnivores that eat the primary consumers. **Tertiary consumers** eat the secondary consumer. These trophic levels may go higher depending on the ecosystem. **Decomposers** are consumers that feed off animal waste and dead organisms. This pathway of food transfer is known as the food chain.

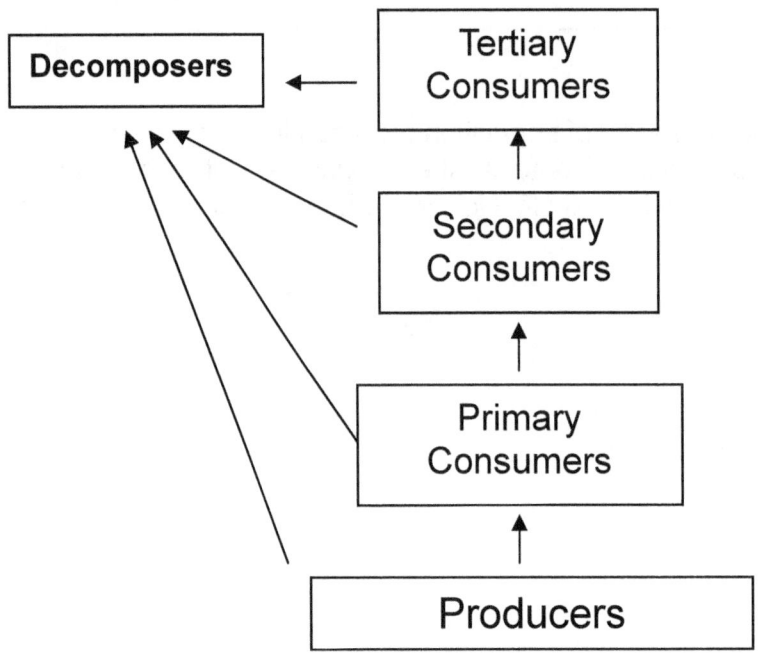

Most food chains are more elaborate, becoming food webs.

COMPETENCY 10.0 UNDERSTAND THE EFFECT OF HUMANS ON THE ENVIRONMENT

Skill 10.1 Identify sources of environmental pollutants

Pollution includes environmental **contamination by chemical, physical, biological, and radioactive substances**. Major types of pollution include:

Air pollution- The release of a variety of chemicals and particulates causes air pollution. These include carbon monoxide, sulfur dioxide and chlorofluorocarbons (CFC's) as well as carbon particulates. The release of compounds derived from sulfur and nitrogen impurities in fossil fuels contribute to air pollution. Smog is a particular type of air pollution caused by a reaction between sunlight and compounds, such as nitrogen oxide and volatile organic compounds, which leads to the brown haze observed over large cities.

Water pollution- Contaminants enter the water system either by ground runoff or by leaching. Historically, industrial waste was dumped directly into bodies of water, but this is more regulated now. However, agricultural runoff continues to pollute water supplies. Buried waste, such as that in landfills, may also leach harmful substances into the soil and groundwater.

Thermal pollution- While industrial facilities typically no longer dispose of contaminants into bodies of water, they may dump water at high temperatures back into the environment. The very hot water both increases temperatures above normal and decreases the concentration of dissolved gases, since gases are less soluble in warm water. Both these effects are disruptive to the local ecosystem.

Radioactive contamination- Radioactive waste from medical, research, and power plant facilities has not always been carefully handled. Accidental leakage and failure to adequately contain waste has led to radioactive pollution in both water and soil.

In addition to certain processes releasing these contaminants into the environment, there are secondary effects in many cases. For instance, many harmful effects have resulted from the combustion of fossil fuels to produce energy for industrial, commercial, and residential facilities as well as to power many types of automobiles. If pure hydrocarbons are burned in oxygen, the only products of combustion are carbon dioxide and water. However, combustion is typically done in air so nitrogen is also present during the reaction resulting in the formation of nitrous oxides. Impurities in the fuel itself mean that compounds such as sulfur dioxide are also formed during combustion. Finally, incomplete combustion releases carbon monoxide. The following are a few of the known detrimental effects of fossil fuel combustion:

Greenhouse gases- While many "greenhouse gases" such as carbon dioxide and nitrous oxide are naturally occurring, their concentration in the atmosphere has dramatically increased as result of fossil fuel use. Greenhouse gases absorb and trap heat, thus warming the planet and possibly triggering climate change.

Acid rain- Sulfur and nitrous oxides are converted to sulfuric and nitric acid in rain. At sufficient concentrations, they will significantly lower the pH of the rain. This acid rain damages man-made and natural structures. Worse yet, it contaminates our planet's water supplies, damaging not only lakes and rivers and their ecosystems but also groundwater and forests.

Skill 10.2 Analyze the effects of humans on natural processes and environments

An important topic in science is the effect of natural disasters and events on society and the effect human activity has on inducing such events. Naturally occurring geological, weather, and environmental events can greatly affect the lives of humans. In addition, the activities of humans can induce such events that would not normally occur.

Nature-induced hazards include floods, landslides, avalanches, volcanic eruptions, wildfires, earthquakes, hurricanes, tornadoes, droughts, and disease. Such events often occur naturally, because of changing weather patterns or geological conditions. Property damage, resource destruction, and the loss of human life are the possible outcomes of natural hazards. Thus, natural hazards are often extremely costly on both an economic and personal level.

While many nature-induced hazards occur naturally, human activity can often stimulate such events. For example, destructive land use practices such as mining can induce landslides or avalanches if not properly planned and monitored. In addition, human activities can cause other hazards including global warming and waste contamination. Global warming is an increase in the Earth's average temperature resulting, at least in part, from the burning of fuels by humans. Global warming is hazardous because it disrupts the Earth's environmental balance and can negatively affect weather patterns. Ecological and weather pattern changes can promote the natural disasters listed above. Finally, improper hazardous waste disposal by humans can contaminate the environment. One important effect of hazardous waste contamination is the stimulation of disease in human populations. Thus, hazardous waste contamination negatively affects both the environment and the people that live in it.

Skill 10.3   Analyze techniques and procedures for protecting the environment

Environmental degradation is damage to an ecosystem, or the biosphere as a whole, resulting from human activities. The underlying causes of environmental degradation are production of energy and consumer products, human population growth and development, and waste disposal. Production of energy and consumer products pollutes the air and contributes to global warming. In addition, harvesting of natural resources can deplete supplies and damage ecosystems. Growth and development of human communities can diminish natural resource supplies, damage the land, and disrupt natural ecosystems. Finally, improper waste disposal can pollute the land and water supplies.

Scientists and policy makers continually attempt to develop and implement new methods and technologies to reduce or mitigate environmental degradation. Cleaner burning fuels or alternative sources of energy that do not pollute the air potential solutions to the energy production-air pollution trade off. In addition, the treatment and filtering of fuel burning by-products can limit environmental impact. However, both developing alternative energy sources and treating current emissions are costly processes. In a market driven economy, governments and policy makers must provide incentives and implement regulations to encourage and require environmental responsibility.

Growth and development of human communities, while inevitable, requires careful planning and attention to environmental concerns. Governmental regulations are often necessary to limit the affect of growth on surrounding ecosystems. Developers and policy makers must attempt to balance the need for increased housing and construction with the importance of respecting and maintaining biodiversity and ecosystem function.

Finally, improper waste disposal can pollute the land and water. Many human and industrial waste products are highly toxic and can cause irreversible environmental damage. Methods of reducing environmental degradation resulting from waste disposal include careful treatment of sewage and human waste, safe disposal of waste products in properly designed locations, and recycling and reuse of waste products.

SUBAREA III. PHYSICAL SCIENCE

COMPETENCY 11.0 UNDERSTAND THE STRUCTURE AND NATURE OF MATTER

Skill 11.1 Identify the parts of an atom and their characteristics

An atom is a nucleus surrounded by a cloud with moving electrons. The nucleus is the center of the atom. The positive particles inside the nucleus are called protons. The mass of a proton is about 2,000 times that of the mass of an electron. The number of protons in the nucleus of an atom is called the atomic number. All atoms of the same element have the same atomic number. Neutrons are another type of particle in the nucleus. Neutrons and protons have about the same mass, but neutrons have no charge. Neutrons were discovered because scientists observed that not all atoms in neon gas have the same mass. They had identified isotopes. Isotopes of an element have the same number of protons in the nucleus, but have different masses. Neutrons explain the difference in mass. They have mass but no charge.

The mass of matter is measured against a standard mass such as the gram. Scientists measure the mass of an atom by comparing it to that of a standard atom. The result is relative mass. The relative mass of an atom is its mass expressed in terms of the mass of the standard atom. The isotope of the element carbon is the standard atom. It has six (6) neutrons and is called carbon-12. It is assigned a mass of 12 atomic mass units (amu). Therefore, the atomic mass unit (amu) is the standard unit for measuring the mass of an atom. It is equal to the mass of a carbon atom.

The mass number of an atom is the sum of its protons and neutrons. In any element, there is a mixture of isotopes, some having slightly more or slightly fewer protons and neutrons. The atomic mass of an element is an average of the mass numbers of its atoms.

Each atom has an equal number of electrons (negative) and protons (positive). Therefore, atoms are neutral. Electrons orbiting the nucleus occupy energy levels that are arranged in order and the electrons tend to occupy the lowest energy level available. A stable electron arrangement is an atom that has all of its electrons in the lowest possible energy levels. Each energy level holds a maximum number of electrons. However, an atom with more than one level does not hold more than 8 electrons in its outermost shell. This can help explain why chemical reactions occur. Atoms react with each other when their outer levels are unfilled. When atoms either exchange or share electrons with each other, these energy levels become filled and the atom becomes more stable. As an electron gains energy, it moves from one energy level to a higher energy level. The electron can not leave one level until it has enough energy to reach the next level. Excited electrons are electrons that have absorbed energy and have moved farther from the nucleus. Electrons can also lose energy. When they do, they fall to a lower level. However, they can only fall to the lowest level that has room for them. This explains why atoms do not collapse.

Skill 11.2   Identify the physical and chemical characteristics of matter (e.g., density, mass, volume, state, reactivity)

Everything in our world is made up of matter, whether it is a rock, a building, an animal, or a person. Matter is defined by its characteristics. It takes up space and it has mass. Mass is a measure of the amount of matter in an object. Two objects of equal mass will balance each other on a simple balance scale no matter where the scale is located. For instance, two rocks with the same amount of mass that are in balance on earth will also be in balance on the moon. They will feel heavier on earth than on the moon because of the gravitational pull of the earth. So, although the two rocks have the same mass, they will have different weight. Weight is the measure of the earth's pull of gravity on an object. It can also be defined as the pull of gravity between other bodies. The units of weight measure that we commonly use are the pound in English measure and the kilogram in metric measure. In addition to mass, matter also has the property of volume.

Volume is the amount of cubic space that an object occupies. Volume and mass together give a more exact description of the object. Two objects may have the same volume, but different mass, the same mass but different volumes, etc. For instance, consider two cubes that are each one cubic centimeter, one made from plastic, one from lead. They have the same volume, but the lead cube has more mass. The measure that we use to describe the cubes takes into consideration both the mass and the volume.

Density is the mass of a substance contained per unit of volume. If the density of an object is less than the density of a liquid, the object will float in the liquid. If the object is denser than the liquid, then the object will sink. Density is stated in grams per cubic centimeter (g / cm3) where the gram is the standard unit of mass. To find an object's density, you must measure its mass and its volume, then divide the mass by the volume (D = m / V). To find an object's density, first use a balance to find its mass. Then calculate its volume. If the object is a regular shape, you can find the volume by multiplying the length, width, and height together. However, if it is an irregular shape, you can find the volume by seeing how much water it displaces. Measure the water in the container before and after the object is submerged. The difference will be the volume of the object.

Specific gravity is the ratio of the density of a substance to the density of water. For instance, the specific density of one liter of turpentine is calculated by comparing its mass (0.81 kg) to the mass of one liter of water (1 kg):

$$\frac{\text{mass of 1 L alcohol}}{\text{mass of 1 L water}} = \frac{0.81 \text{ kg}}{1.00 \text{ kg}} = 0.81$$

Physical properties and chemical properties of matter describe the appearance or behavior of a substance. A physical property can be observed without changing the identity of a substance. For instance, you can describe the color, mass, shape, and volume of a book. Chemical properties describe the ability of a substance to be changed into new substances. Baking powder goes through a chemical change as it changes into carbon dioxide gas during the baking process. Matter constantly changes. A physical change is a change that does not produce a new substance. The freezing and melting of water is an example of physical change. A chemical change (or chemical reaction) is any change of a substance into one or more other substances. Burning materials turn into smoke, a seltzer tablet fizzes into gas bubbles.

TEACHER CERTIFICATION STUDY GUIDE

Skill 11.2 Recognize types and characteristics of chemical bonding and its relationship to molecular structures

The outermost electrons in the atoms are called valence electrons. Because they are the ones involved in the bonding process, they determine the properties of the element.

A **chemical bond** is a force of attraction that holds atoms together. When atoms are bonded chemically, they cease to have their individual properties. For instance, hydrogen and oxygen combine into water and no longer look like hydrogen and oxygen. They look like water.

A **covalent bond** is formed when two atoms share electrons. Recall that atoms whose outer shells are not filled with electrons are unstable. When they are unstable, they readily combine with other unstable atoms. By combining and sharing electrons, they act as a single unit. Covalent bonding happens among nonmetals. Covalent bonds are always polar when between two non-identical atoms. Covalent compounds are compounds whose atoms are joined by covalent bonds. Table sugar, methane, and ammonia are examples of covalent compounds.

An **ionic bond** is a bond formed by the transfer of electrons. It happens when metals and nonmetals bond. Before chlorine and sodium combine, the sodium has one valence electron and chlorine has seven. Neither valence shell is filled, but the chlorine's valence shell is almost full. During the reaction, the sodium gives one valence electron to the chlorine atom. Both atoms then have filled shells and are stable. Something else has happened during the bonding. Before the bonding, both atoms were neutral. When one electron was transferred, it upset the balance of protons and electrons in each atom. The chlorine atom took on one extra electron and the sodium atom released one electron. The atoms have now become ions. Ions are atoms with an unequal number of protons and electrons. To determine whether the ion is positive or negative, compare the number of protons (+charge) to the electrons (-charge). If there are more electrons the ion will be negative. If there are more protons, the ion will be positive. Compounds that result from the transfer of metal atoms to nonmetal atoms are called ionic compounds. Sodium chloride (table salt), sodium hydroxide (drain cleaner), and potassium chloride (salt substitute) are examples of ionic compounds.

Skill 11.3 Use the kinetic molecular model, the periodic table of the elements, and other models of atomic structure to explain and predict the behavior of matter

Gas **pressure** results from molecular collisions with container walls. The **number of molecules** striking an **area** on the walls and the **average kinetic energy** per molecule are the only factors that contribute to pressure. A higher **temperature** increases speed and kinetic energy. There are more collisions at higher temperatures, but the average distance between molecules does not change, and thus density does not change in a sealed container.

Kinetic molecular theory (KMT) explains how the pressure and temperature influences behavior of gases by making a few assumptions, namely:

1) The energies of intermolecular attractive and repulsive forces may be neglected.
2) The average kinetic energy of the molecules is proportional to absolute temperature.
3) Energy can be transferred between molecules during collisions and the collisions are elastic, so the average kinetic energy of the molecules doesn't change due to collisions.
4) The volume of all molecules in a gas is negligible compared to the total volume of the container.

Strictly speaking, molecules also contain some kinetic energy by rotating or experiencing other motions. The motion of a molecule from one place to another is called **translation**. Translational kinetic energy is the form that is transferred by collisions, and kinetic molecular theory ignores other forms of kinetic energy because they are not proportional to temperature.

Molecules have **kinetic energy** (they move around), and they also have **intermolecular attractive forces** (they stick to each other). The relationship between these two determines whether a collection of molecules will be a gas, liquid, or solid.

A **gas** has an indefinite shape and an indefinite volume. The kinetic model for a gas is a collection of widely separated molecules, each moving in a random and free fashion, with negligible attractive or repulsive forces between them. Gases will expand to occupy a larger container so there is more space between the molecules. Gases can also be compressed to fit into a small container so the molecules are less separated. **Diffusion** occurs when one material spreads into or through another. Gases diffuse rapidly and move from one place to another.

A **liquid** assumes the shape of the portion of any container that it occupies and has a specific volume. The kinetic model for a liquid is a collection of molecules attracted to each other with sufficient strength to keep them close to each other but with insufficient strength to prevent them from moving around randomly. Liquids have a higher density and are much less compressible than gases because the molecules in a liquid are closer together. Diffusion occurs more slowly in liquids than in gases because the molecules in a liquid stick to each other and are not completely free to move.

A **solid** has a definite volume and definite shape. The kinetic model for a solid is a collection of molecules attracted to each other with sufficient strength to essentially lock them in place. Each molecule may vibrate, but it has an average position relative to its neighbors. If these positions form an ordered pattern, the solid is called **crystalline**. Otherwise, it is called **amorphous**. Solids have a high density and are almost incompressible because the molecules are close together. Diffusion occurs extremely slowly because the molecules almost never alter their position.

In a solid, the energy of intermolecular attractive forces is much stronger than the kinetic energy of the molecules, so kinetic energy and kinetic molecular theory are not very important. As temperature increases in a solid, the vibrations of individual molecules grow more intense and the molecules spread slightly further apart, decreasing the density of the solid.

In a liquid, the energy of intermolecular attractive forces is about as strong as the kinetic energy of the molecules and both play a role in the properties of liquids.

In a gas, the energy of intermolecular forces is much weaker than the kinetic energy of the molecules. Kinetic molecular theory is usually applied for gases and is best applied by imagining ourselves shrinking down to become a molecule and picturing what happens when we bump into other molecules and into container walls.

COMPETENCY 12.0 UNDERSTAND PHYSICAL AND CHEMICAL CHANGES AND CHEMICAL REACTIONS

Skill 12.1 Distinguish between physical and chemical changes and their characteristics

A **physical change** does not create a new substance. **Atoms are not rearranged into different compounds**. The material has the same chemical composition as it had before the change. Changes of state as described in the previous section are physical changes. Frozen water or gaseous water is still H_2O. Taking a piece of paper and tearing it up is a physical change. You simply have smaller pieces of paper.

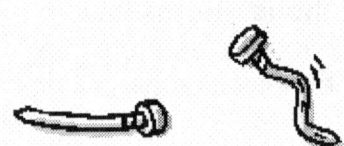

Compare these two nails....They are still iron nails, made of iron atoms. The difference is that one is bent while the other is straight. This is a physical change.

A **chemical change** is a chemical reaction. It **converts one substance into another** because atoms are rearranged to form a different compound. Paper undergoes a chemical change when you burn it. You no longer have paper. A chemical change to a pure substance alters its properties.

An iron nail rusts to form a rusty nail. The rusty nail, however, is not made up of the same iron atoms. It is now composed of iron (III) oxide molecules that form when the iron atoms combine with oxygen molecules during oxidation (rusting).

Skill 12.2 Analyze types of chemical reactions and their characteristics

There are four kinds of chemical reactions:

In a **composition reaction**, two or more substances combine to form a compound.

$A + B \rightarrow AB$
i.e. silver and sulfur yield silver dioxide

MID. LEVEL SCIENCE   50

In a **decomposition reaction**, a compound breaks down into two or more simpler substances.

AB → A + B
i.e. water breaks down into hydrogen and oxygen

In a **single replacement reaction**, a free element replaces an element that is part of a compound.

A + BX → AX + B
i.e. iron plus copper sulfate yields iron sulfate plus copper

In a **double replacement reaction**, parts of two compounds replace each other. In this case, the compounds seem to switch partners.

AX + BY → AY + BX
i.e. sodium chloride plus mercury nitrate yields sodium nitrate plus mercury chloride.

Skill 12.3   Interpret notation used to represent chemical reactions

Let us look at the chemical formula for aerobic respiration. Our tissues need energy for growth, repair, movement, excretion, and so on. This energy is obtained from glucose supplied to the tissues by our blood. In aerobic respiration, glucose is broken down in the presence of oxygen into carbon dioxide and water and energy is released, which is used for our metabolic processes.   This reaction can be written in the form of a word reaction:

Glucose + Oxygen = Carbon Dioxide + Water + Energy

By using chemical symbols and subscripts we can rewrite the above word equation into a proper chemical equation:

$C_6H_{12}O_6 + 6O_2 = 6CO_2 + 6H_2O +$ Energy

The compounds on the left side of the equation are called reactants and the compounds on the right side of the reaction are called products. The reactants in the above equation have to combine in a fixed proportion for a chemical reaction to take place.

COMPETENCY 13.0 UNDERSTAND THE BASIC CONCEPTS OF FORCE, WORK, AND MOTION

Skill 13.1 Identify types and characteristics of force, work, and motion

Dynamics is the study of the relationship between motion and the forces affecting motion. **Force** causes motion.

Mass and weight are not the same quantities. An object's **mass** gives it a reluctance to change its current state of motion. It is also the measure of an object's resistance to acceleration. The force that the earth's gravity exerts on an object with a specific mass is called the object's weight on earth. Weight is a force that is measured in Newtons. Weight (W) = mass times acceleration due to gravity. **(W = mg)**. To illustrate the difference between mass and weight, picture two rocks of equal mass on a balance scale. If the scale is balanced in one place, it will be balanced everywhere, regardless of the gravitational field. However, the weight of the stones would vary on a spring scale, depending upon the gravitational field. In other words, the stones would be balanced both on earth and on the moon. However, the weight of the stones would be greater on earth than on the moon.

Newton's laws of motion:

Newton's first law of motion is also called the law of inertia. It states that an object at rest will remain at rest and an object in motion will remain in motion at a constant velocity unless acted upon by an external force.

Newton's second law of motion states that if a net force acts on an object, it will cause the acceleration of the object. The relationship between force and motion is Force equals mass times acceleration. **(F = ma).**

Newton's third law states that for every action there is an equal and opposite reaction. Therefore, if an object exerts a force on another object, that second object exerts an equal and opposite force on the first.

Surfaces that touch each other have a certain resistance to motion. This resistance is **friction.**

Work is done on an object when an applied force moves through a distance.

Power is the work done divided by the amount of time that it took to do it. (Power = Work / time)

MID. LEVEL SCIENCE

Skill 13.2   Identify the forces affecting an object in a given situation

Push and pulls –Pushing a volleyball or pulling a bowstring applies muscular force when the muscles expand and contract. When the bow is released, it is elastic force when any object returns to its original shape.

Rubbing – Friction opposes the motion of one surface past another. Friction is common when slowing down a car.

Pull of gravity – is a force of attraction between two objects. Gravity questions can be raised not only on earth but also between planets and even black hole discussions.

Forces on objects at rest – The formula $F= m/a$ means that a force equals mass over acceleration. An object will not move unless the force is strong enough to move the mass. Also there can be opposing forces holding the object in place. For instance a boat may want to be forced by the currents to drift away but an equal and opposite force is a rope holding it to a dock.

Forces on a moving object - Overcoming inertia is the tendency of any object to oppose a change in motion. An object at rest tends to stay at rest. An object that is moving tends to keep moving.

Inertia and circular motion – The centripetal force is provided by the high banking of the curved road and by friction between the wheels and the road. This inward force keeps an object moving in a circle is centripetal force.

Skill 13.3   Apply physical laws to interpret and predict the motion of objects

A **free-body diagram** is a diagram that shows the direction and relative magnitude of forces acting upon an object in a given situation. It is a special example of a vector diagram. The direction of the arrow indicates the direction in which the force is acting, and the size of the arrow indicates the magnitude of the force. Each arrow is labeled to represent the exact type of force. A box is used to represent the object and the force arrows are drawn outward from the center of the box in the directions they are acting.

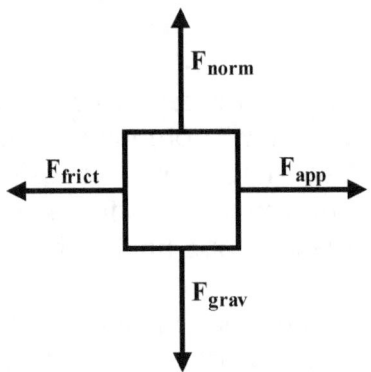

In this example, the object has four forces acting upon it, which is not always the case. Sometimes, there could be one, two, or three forces. The only rule is that all forces acting upon the object in that given situation should be depicted. Therefore, it is important that you be familiar with the various types of forces and be able to identify which forces are present in the situation.

The science of describing the motion of bodies is known as **kinematics**. The motion of bodies is described using words, diagrams, numbers, graphs, and equations.

The following words are used to describe motion: vectors, scalars, distance, displacement, speed, velocity, and acceleration.

The two categories of mathematical quantities that are used to describe the motion of objects are scalars and vectors. **Scalars** are quantities that are fully described by magnitude alone. Examples of scalars are 5m and 20 degrees Celsius. **Vectors** are quantities that are fully described by magnitude and direction. Examples of vectors are 30m/sec, and 5 miles north.

Distance is a scalar quantity that refers to how much ground an object has covered while moving. **Displacement** is a vector quantity that refers to the object's change in position.

Example:

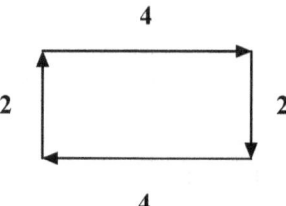

Jamie walked 2 miles north, 4 miles east, 2 miles south, and then 4 miles west. In terms of distance, she walked 12 miles. However, there is no displacement because the directions cancelled each other out, and she returned to her starting position.

Speed is a scalar quantity that refers to how fast an object is moving (ex. the car was traveling 60 mi./hr). **Velocity** is a vector quantity that refers to the rate at which an object changes its position. In other words, velocity is speed with direction (ex. the car was traveling 60 mi/hr east).

$$\text{Average speed} = \frac{\text{Distance traveled}}{\text{Time of travel}}$$

$$v = \frac{d}{t}$$

$$\text{Average velocity} = \frac{\Delta \text{position}}{\text{time}} = \frac{\text{displacement}}{\text{time}}$$

Instantaneous Speed - speed at any given instant in time.

Average Speed - average of all instantaneous speeds, found simply by a distance/time ratio.

Acceleration is a vector quantity defined as the rate at which an object changes its velocity.

$$a = \frac{\Delta velocity}{time} = \frac{v_f - v_i}{t}$$ where *f* represents the final velocity and *i* represents the initial velocity

Since acceleration is a vector quantity, it always has a direction associated with it. The direction of the acceleration vector depends on

- whether the object is speeding up or slowing down
- whether the object is moving in the positive or negative direction.

Projectile Motion

By definition, a **projectile** only has one force acting upon it – the force of gravity.

Gravity influences the vertical motion of the projectile, causing vertical acceleration. The horizontal motion of the projectile is the result of the tendency of any object in motion to remain in motion at constant velocity. (Remember, there are no horizontal forces acting upon the projectile. By definition, gravity is the only force acting upon the projectile.)

Projectiles travel with a parabolic trajectory due to the fact that the downward force of gravity accelerates them downward from their otherwise straight-line trajectory. Gravity affects the vertical motion, not the horizontal motion, of the projectile. Gravity causes a downward displacement from the position that the object would be in if there were no gravity.

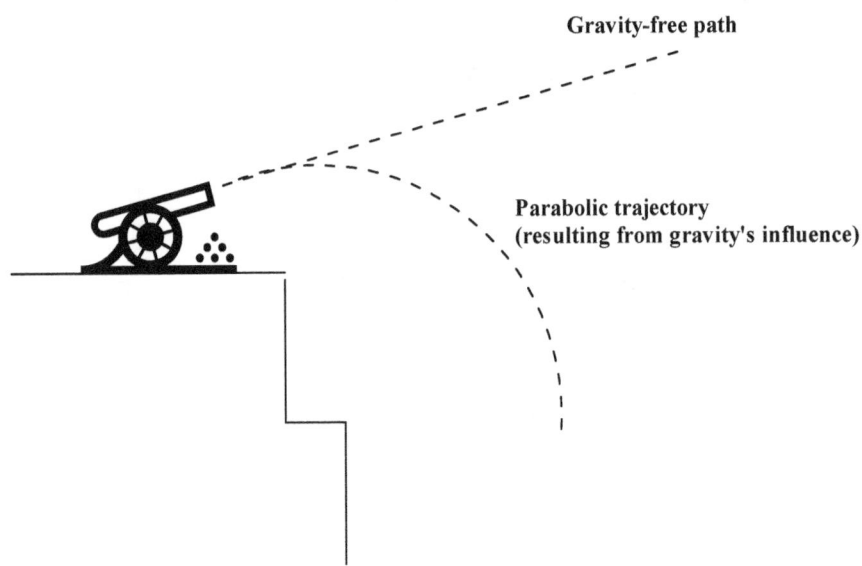

Pendulum

A simple pendulum consists of a weight or bob suspended at the end of a string from a fixed point so that it can swing back and forth under the influence of gravity. The period, or cycle, of the motion, is the time it takes for the pendulum to make a complete trip from one side to the other. You can make the period of the motion of the pendulum shorter or longer by shortening or lengthening the length of the string, but the motion remains constant. Changing the mass of the weight or bob alone will not change the period of the motion.

COMPETENCY 14.0 UNDERSTAND ENERGY AND ITS FORMS AND TRANSFORMATIONS

Skill 14.1 Identify forms of energy (e.g., electrical, mechanical, heat, nuclear) and their characteristics

The law of conservation of energy states that energy is neither created nor destroyed. Thus, energy changes form when energy transactions occur in nature. The following are the major forms energy can take.

Thermal energy is the total internal energy of objects created by the vibration and movement of atoms and molecules. Heat is the transfer of thermal energy.
Acoustical energy, or sound energy, is the movement of energy through an object in waves. Energy that forces an object to vibrate creates sound.
Radiant energy is the energy of electromagnetic waves. Light, visible and otherwise, is an example of radiant energy.
Electrical energy is the movement of electrical charges in an electromagnetic field. Examples of electrical energy are electricity and lightning.
Chemical energy is the energy stored in the chemical bonds of molecules. For example, the energy derived from gasoline is chemical energy.
Mechanical energy is the potential and kinetic energy of a mechanical system. Rolling balls, car engines, and body parts in motion exemplify mechanical energy.
Nuclear energy is the energy present in the nucleus of atoms. Division, combination, or collision of nuclei release nuclear energy.

Because the total energy in the universe is constant, energy continually transitions between forms. For example, an engine burns gasoline converting the chemical energy of the gasoline into mechanical energy, a plant converts radiant energy of the sun into chemical energy found in glucose, or a battery converts chemical energy into electrical energy.

Skill 14.2 Recognize the conservation of energy in various situations

One of the universal laws is the conservation of matter. This means that everything in the universe remains constant, although its form may change. Nothing is created or destroyed, but is instead indefinitely recycled, either in substance or energy.

For example, conservation of mass in nature includes the burning of wood, rusting of iron, and phase changes of matter. When wood burns, the total mass of the products, such as soot, ash, and gases, equals the mass of the wood and the oxygen that reacts with it. When iron reacts with oxygen, rust forms. The total mass of the iron-rust complex does not change. Finally, when matter changes phase, mass remains constant. Thus, when a glacier melts due to atmospheric warming, the mass of liquid water formed is equal to the mass of the glacier.

In chemistry we work with the conservation of energy. In chemical reactions and interactions of charged objects, the total charge does not change. The left (reactants) and right sides (products) of the equation remain equal. This is often accomplished through an adjustment in energy. Chemical reactions and the interaction of charged molecules are essential and common processes in living organisms and systems.

Skill 14.3   Identify and analyze energy transfers and conversions

Thermodynamics is the study of energy and energy transfer. The first law of thermodynamics states the energy of the universe is constant. Thus, interactions involving energy deal with the transfer and transformation of energy, not the creation or destruction of energy.

Electricity is an important source of energy. Ovens and electric heaters convert electrical energy into heat energy. Electrical energy energizes the filament of a light bulb to produce light. Finally, the movement of electrical charges creates magnetic fields. Charges moving in a magnetic field experience a force, which is a transfer of energy.

The process of photosynthesis converts light energy from the sun into chemical energy (sugar). Cellular respiration later converts the sugar into ATP, a major energy source of all living organisms. Plants and certain types of bacteria carry out photosynthesis. The actions of the green pigment chlorophyll allow the conversion of unusable light energy into usable chemical energy.

Energy transfer plays an important role in weather processes. The three main types of heat transfer to the atmosphere are radiation, conduction, and convection. Radiation is the transfer of heat by electromagnetic waves. Sun light is an example of radiation. Conduction is the transfer of energy from one substance to another, or within a substance. Convection is the transfer of heat energy in a fluid. Air in the atmosphere acts as a fluid for the transfer of heat energy. Convection, resulting indirectly from the energy generated by sun light, is responsible for many weather phenomena including wind and clouds.

Energy transfer is also a key concept in the creation of food webs and food pyramids. Food webs and pyramids show the feeding relationships between organisms in an ecosystem. The primary producers of an ecosystem produce organic compounds from an energy source and inorganic materials. Primary consumers obtain energy by feeding on producers. Finally, secondary consumers obtain energy by feeding on primary consumers.

Skill 14.4 Recognize the relationship between kinetic and potential energy

Mechanical energy is the potential and kinetic energy of a mechanical system. Rolling balls, car engines, and body parts in motion exemplify mechanical energy. Interacting objects in the universe constantly exchange and transform energy. Total energy remains the same, but the form of the energy readily changes. Energy exists in two basic forms, potential and kinetic. Kinetic energy is the energy of a moving object. Potential energy is the energy stored in matter due to position relative to other objects. Energy often changes from kinetic (motion) to potential (stored) or in the opposite direction from potential to kinetic.

In any object, solid, liquid or gas, the atoms and molecules that make up the object are constantly moving (vibrational, translation and rotational motion) and colliding with each other. They are not stationary.

Due to this motion, the object's particles have varying amounts of kinetic energy. A fast moving atom can push a slower moving atom during a collision, so it has energy. All moving objects have energy and that energy depends on the object's mass and velocity. Kinetic energy is calculated: K.E. = $\frac{1}{2} mv^2$.

The temperature exhibited by an object is proportional to the average kinetic energy of the particles in the substance. Increase the temperature of a substance and its particles move faster so their average kinetic energies increase as well. But temperature is NOT an energy; it is not conserved.

The energy an object has due to its position or arrangement of its parts is called potential energy. Potential energy due to position is equal to the mass of the object times the gravitational pull on the object times the height of the object, or **PE = mgh,** Where PE = potential energy; m = mass of object; g = gravity; and h = height.

Heat is energy that is transferred between objects caused by differences in their temperatures. Heat passes spontaneously from an object of higher temperature to one of lower temperature. This transfer continues until both objects reach the same temperature. Both kinetic energy and potential energy can be transformed into heat energy. When you step on the brakes in your car, the kinetic energy of the car is changed to heat energy by friction between the brake and the wheels. Other transformations can occur from kinetic to potential as well. Since most of the energy in our world is in a form that is not easily used, man and Mother Nature has developed some clever ways of changing one form of energy into another form that may be more useful.

COMPETENCY 15.0 UNDERSTAND WAVES, SOUND, AND LIGHT

Skill 15.1 Use terms associated with waves, sound, and light (e.g., frequency, amplitude, wavelength, pitch, loudness, color)

The **pitch** of a sound depends on the **frequency** that the ear receives. High-pitched sound waves have high frequencies. High notes are produced by an object that is vibrating at a greater number of times per second than one that produces a low note.

The **intensity** of a sound is the amount of energy that crosses a unit of area in a given unit of time. The loudness of the sound is subjective and depends upon the effect on the human ear. Two tones of the same intensity but different pitches may appear to have different loudness. The intensity level of sound is measured in decibels. Normal conversation is about 60 decibels. A power saw is about 110 decibels.

The **amplitude** of a sound wave determines its loudness. Loud sound waves have large amplitudes. The larger the sound wave, the more energy is needed to create the wave.

Light, microwaves, x-rays, and TV and radio transmissions are all kinds of electromagnetic waves. They are all a wavy disturbance that repeats itself over a distance called the **wavelength**. Electromagnetic waves come in varying sizes and properties, by which they are organized in the electromagnetic spectrum. The electromagnetic spectrum is measured in frequency (f) in hertz and wavelength (λ) in meters. The frequency times the wavelength of every electromagnetic wave equals the speed of light (3.0×10^9 meters/second).

Skill 15.2 Identify phenomena related to waves, sound, and light (e.g., reflection, refraction, shadows, echoes)

When light hits a surface, it is **reflected.** The angle of the incoming light (angle of incidence) is the same as the angle of the reflected light (angle of reflection). It is this reflected light that allows you to see objects. You see the objects when the reflected light reaches your eyes.

Different surfaces reflect light differently. Rough surfaces scatter light in many different directions. A smooth surface reflects the light in one direction. If it is smooth and shiny (like a mirror) you see your image in the surface.

When light enters a different medium, it bends. This bending, or change of speed, is called **refraction**.

MID. LEVEL SCIENCE

Shadows illustrate one of the basic properties of light. Light travels in a straight line. If you put your hand between a light source and a wall, you will interrupt the light and produce a shadow.

Change in experienced frequency due to relative motion of the source of the sound is called the **Doppler Effect**. When a siren approaches, the pitch is high. When it passes, the pitch drops. As a moving sound source approaches a listener, the sound waves are closer together, causing an increase in frequency in the sound that is heard. As the source passes the listener, the waves spread out and the frequency experienced by the listener is lower.

An **echo** is a wave that has been reflected by a medium, and returns to your ear. The delay between its reflection and your perception of its return is equal to the distance divided by the speed of sound.

Skill 15.3 Analyze given situations in terms of the behavior of waves, sound, and light

The place where one medium ends and another begins is called a **boundary**, and the manner in which a wave behaves when it reaches that boundary is called **boundary behavior**. The following principles apply to boundary behavior in waves:

1) wave speed is always greater in the less dense medium
2) wavelength is always greater in the less dense medium
3) wave frequency is not changed by crossing a boundary
4) the reflected pulse becomes inverted when a wave in a less dense medium is heading towards a boundary with a more dense medium
5) the amplitude of the incident pulse is always greater than the amplitude of the reflected pulse.

For an example, we will use a rope whose left side is less dense, or thinner, than the right side of the rope.

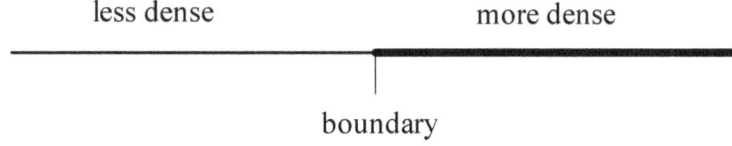

Sound waves need a medium in which to spread; light waves do not. The speed of any wave depends upon the elastic and inertial properties of the medium through which it travels. The density of a medium is an example of an **inertial property**. Sound usually travels faster in denser material. A sound wave will travel nearly three times as fast through helium than through air. On the other hand, the speed of light is slower in denser materials. The speed of light is slower in glass than in air. (The standard for the speed of light, c, is actually the speed of light in a vacuum, such as empty space.)

Elastic properties are properties related to the tendency of a medium to maintain its shape when acted upon by force or stress. Sound waves travel faster in solids than they do in liquids, and faster in liquids than they do in gases. The inertial factor would seem to indicate otherwise. However, the elastic factor has a greater influence on the speed of the wave.

When a wave strikes an object, some of the wave energy is reflected off the object, some of the energy goes into and is absorbed by the object, and some of the energy goes through the object. For example, sound waves can penetrate walls. However, sound waves from the air cannot penetrate water, and sound waves from water cannot penetrate the air. Light passes through some materials such as glass but not many other materials.

COMPETENCY 16.0 UNDERSTAND ELECTRICITY, MAGNETS, AND ELECTROMAGNETISM

Skill 16.1 Identify the characteristics of static electricity, current electricity, and electric circuits

An **electric circuit** is a path along which electrons flow. A simple circuit can be created with a dry cell, wire, a bell, or a light bulb. When all are connected, the electrons flow from the negative terminal, through the wire to the device and back to the positive terminal of the dry cell. If there are no breaks in the circuit, the device will work. The circuit is closed. Any break in the flow will create an open circuit and cause the device to shut off.

The device (bell, bulb) is an example of a **load**. A load is a device that uses energy. Suppose that you also add a buzzer so that the bell rings when you press the buzzer button. The buzzer is acting as a **switch**. A switch is a device that opens or closes a circuit. Pressing the buzzer makes the connection complete and the bell rings. When the buzzer is not engaged, the circuit is open and the bell is silent.

A **series circuit** is one where the electrons have only one path along which they can move. When one load in a series circuit goes out, the circuit is open. An example of this is a set of Christmas tree lights that is missing a bulb. None of the bulbs will work.

A **parallel circuit** is one where the electrons have more than one path to move along. If a load goes out in a parallel circuit, the other load will still work because the electrons can still find a way to continue moving along the path.

Static electricity is created when an object gives up or gains electrons. The most common example is that rubbing wool over something made of plastic/rubber gives that object a positive charge. The wool gives up its electrons to the plastic/rubber. This charge is called "static" because it is not moving along a conductor.

Skill 16.2 Analyze the relationship between electricity and magnetism

A magnet can be made out of a coil of wire by connecting the ends of the coil to a battery. When the current goes through the wire, the wire acts in the same way that a magnet does, it is called an **electromagnet**. The poles of the electromagnet will depend upon which way the electric current runs. An electromagnet can be made more powerful in three ways:

1. Make more coils.
2. Put an iron core (nail) inside the coils.
3. Use more battery power.

In a **motor**, electricity is used to create magnetic fields that oppose each other and cause the rotor to move. The wiring loops attached to the rotating shaft have a magnetic field opposing the magnetic field caused by the wiring in the housing of the motor that cannot move. The repelling action of the opposing magnetic fields turns the rotor.

A **generator** is a device that turns rotary mechanical energy into electrical energy. The process is based on the relationship between magnetism and electricity. As a wire or any other conductor moves across a magnetic field, an electric current occurs in the wire. The large generators used by the electric companies have a stationary conductor. A magnet attached to the end of a rotating shaft is positioned inside a stationary conducting ring that is wrapped with a long, continuous piece of wire. When the magnet rotates, it induces a small electric current in each section of wire as it passes. Each section of wire is a small, separate electric conductor. All the small currents of these individual sections add up to one large current, which is what is used for electric power.

Skill 16.3   Demonstrate knowledge of the characteristics of magnets and magnetic fields

Magnets have a north pole and a south pole. Like poles repel and opposing poles attract. A **magnetic field** is the space around a magnet where its force will affect objects. The closer you are to a magnet, the stronger the force. As you move away, the force becomes weaker.

Some materials act as magnets and some do not. This is because magnetism is a result of electrons in motion. The most important motion in this case is the spinning of the individual electrons. Electrons spin in pairs in opposite directions in most atoms. Each spinning electron has the magnetic field that it creates canceled out by the electron that is spinning in the opposite direction.

In an atom of iron, there are four unpaired electrons. The magnetic fields of these are not canceled out. Their fields add up to make a tiny magnet. Their fields exert forces on each other setting up small areas in the iron called **magnetic domains** where atomic magnetic fields line up in the same direction.

You can make a magnet out of an iron nail by stroking the nail in the same direction repeatedly with a magnet. This causes poles in the atomic magnets in the nail to be attracted to the magnet. The tiny magnetic fields in the nail line up in the direction of the magnet. The magnet causes the domains pointing in its direction to grow in the nail. Eventually, one large domain results and the nail becomes a magnet.

A bar magnet has a north pole and a south pole. If you break the magnet in half, each piece will have a north and south pole.

The earth has a magnetic field. In a compass, a tiny, lightweight magnet is suspended and will line its south pole up with the North Pole magnet of the earth.

SUBAREA IV. **EARTH AND SPACE SCIENCE**

COMPETENCY 17.0 UNDERSTAND GEOLOGY AND GEOLOGIC HISTORY

Skill 17.1 Identify characteristics of rocks, minerals, and soils and the processes by which they form (e.g., rock cycle)

Three major subdivisions of rocks are sedimentary, metamorphic and igneous.

Lithification of sedimentary rocks

When fluid sediments are transformed into solid sedimentary rocks, the process is known as lithification. One very common process affecting sediments is compaction where the weights of overlying materials compress and compact the deeper sediments. The compaction process leads to cementation. Cementation is when sediments are converted to sedimentary rock.

Igneous rocks

Igneous rocks can be classified according to their texture, their composition, and the way they formed. Molten rock is called magma. When molten rock pours out onto the surface of Earth, it is called lava. As magma cools, the elements and compounds begin to form crystals. The slower the magma cools, the larger the crystals grow. Rocks with large crystals are said to have a coarse-grained texture. Granite is an example of a coarse grained rock. Rocks that cool rapidly before any crystals can form have a glassy texture such as obsidian, also commonly known as volcanic glass.

Metamorphic rocks

Metamorphic rocks are formed by high temperatures and great pressures. The process by which the rocks undergo these changes is called metamorphism. The outcome of metamorphic changes include deformation by extreme heat and pressure, compaction, destruction of the original characteristics of the parent rock, bending and folding while in a plastic stage, and the emergence of completely new and different minerals due to chemical reactions with heated water and dissolved minerals. Metamorphic rocks are classified into two groups, foliated (leaf like) rocks and unfoliated rocks. Foliated rocks consist of compressed, parallel bands of minerals, which give the rocks a striped appearance. Examples of such rocks include; slate, schist, and gneiss. Unfoliated rocks are not banded and examples of such include; quartzite, marble, and anthracite rocks.

Minerals

Minerals are natural, non-living solids with a definite chemical composition and a crystalline structure. Ores are minerals or rock deposits that can be mined for a profit. Rocks are Earth materials made of one or more minerals. Rock Facies is a rock group that differs from comparable rocks (as in composition, age or fossil content).

Characteristics by which minerals are classified

Minerals must adhere to five criteria. They must be (1) non-living, (2) formed in nature, (3) solid in form, (4) their atoms form a crystalline pattern, (5) Its chemical composition is fixed within narrow limits. There are over 3000 minerals in earth's crust. Minerals are classified by composition. The major groups of minerals are silicates, carbonates, oxides, sulfides, sulfates, and halides. The largest group of minerals is the silicates. Silicates are made of silicon, oxygen, and one or more other elements.

Skill 17.2 Identify the structure and composition of the earth and the interactions among its layers

The earth's physical environment is divided into three major parts: the atmosphere, the hydrosphere, and the lithoshpere: The atmosphere is the layer of air that surrounds the earth. The hydrosphere is the water portion of the planet (70% of the earth is covered by water) and the lithosphere is the solid portion of the earth.

The earth's layered structure includes the core, mantle, and the crust.

Core

The outer core of the Earth begins about 3000 km beneath the surface and is a liquid, though far more viscous than that of the mantle. Even deeper, approximately 5000 beneath the surface is the solid inner core. The inner core has a radius of about 1200 km. Temperatures in the core exceed 4000°C. Scientists agree that the core is extremely dense. This conclusion is based on the fact that the Earth is known to have an average density of 5515 kg/m^3 even though the material close to the surface has an average density of only 3000 kg/m^3. Therefore a denser core must exist. Additionally, it is hypothesized that when the Earth was forming, the densest material sank to the middle of the planet. Thus, it is not surprising that the core is about 80% iron. In fact, there is some speculation that the entire inner core is a single iron crystal, while the outer core is a mix of liquid iron and nickel.

Mantle

The Earth's mantle begins about 35 km beneath the surface and stretches all the way to 3000 km beneath the surface, where the outer core begins. Since the mantle stretches so far into the Earth's center, its temperature varies widely; near the boundary with the crust it is approximately 1000°C, while near the outer core it may reach nearly 4000°C. Within the mantle there are silicate rocks, which are rich in iron and magnesium. The silicate rocks exist as solids, but the high heat means they are ductile enough to "flow" over long time scales. In general, the mantle is semi-solid/plastic and the viscosity varies as pressures and temperatures change at varying depths.

Crust

It is not clear how long the Earth has actually had a solid crust; most of the rocks are less than 100 million years, though some are 4.4 billion years old. The crust of the earth is the outermost layer and continues down for between 5 and 70 km beneath the surface. Thin areas generally exist under ocean basins (oceanic crust) and thicker crust underlies the continents (continental crust). Oceanic crust is composed largely of iron magnesium silicate rocks, while continental crust is less dense and consists mainly of sodium potassium aluminum silicate rocks. The crust is the least dense layer of the Earth and so is rich in those materials that "floated" during Earth's formation. Additionally, some heavier elements that bound to lighter materials are present in the crust.

Interactions between the Layers

It is not the case that these layers exist as separate entities, with little interaction between them. For instance, it is generally believed that swirling of the iron-rich liquid in the outer core results in the Earth's magnetic field, which is readily apparent on the surface. Heat also moves out from the core to the mantle and crust. The core still retains heat from the formation of the Earth and additional heat is generated by the decay of radioactive isotopes. While most of the heat in our atmosphere comes from sun, radiant heat from the core does warm oceans and other large bodies of water.

There is also a great deal of interaction between the mantle and the crust. The slow convection of rocks in the mantle is responsible for the shifting of tectonic plates on the crust. Matter can also move between the layers as occurs during the rock cycle. Within the rock cycle, igneous rocks are formed when magma escapes from the mantle as lava during volcanic eruption. Rocks may also be forced back into the mantle, where the high heat and pressure recreate them as metamorphic rocks.

Interactions among the spheres

While the hydrosphere, lithosphere, and atmosphere can be described and considered separately, they are actually constantly interacting with one another. Energy and matter flows freely between these different spheres. For instance, in the water cycle, water beneath the Earth's surface and in rocks (in the lithosphere) is exchanged with vapor in the atmosphere and liquid water in lakes and the ocean (the hydrosphere). Similarly, significant events in one sphere almost always have effects in the other spheres. The recent increase in greenhouse gases provides an example of this ripple effect. Additional greenhouse gases produced by human activities were released into the atmosphere where they built up and caused widening holes in certain areas of the atmosphere and global warming. These increasing temperatures have had many effects on the hydrosphere: rising sea levels, increasing water temperature, and climate changes. These lead to even more changes in the lithosphere such as glacier retreat and alterations in the patterns of water-rock interaction (run-off, erosion, etc).

Skill 17.3   Analyze processes that produce geologic change and transformation (e.g., tectonic and volcanic activity, uplifting, erosion, glaciation)

Data obtained from many sources led scientists to develop the theory of plate tectonics. This theory is the most current model that explains not only the movement of the continents, but also the changes in the earth's crust caused by internal forces. Plates are rigid blocks of earth's crust and upper mantle. These rigid solid blocks make up the lithosphere. The earth's lithosphere is broken into nine large sections and several small ones. These moving slabs are called plates. The major plates are named after the continents they are transporting. The plates float on and move with a layer of hot, plastic-like rock in the upper mantle. Geologists believe that the heat currents circulating within the mantle cause this plastic zone of rock to slowly flow, carrying along the overlying crustal plates. Movement of these crustal plates creates areas where the plates diverge as well as areas where the plates converge.

In the Mid-Atlantic is a major area of divergence. Currents of hot mantle rock rise and separate at this point of divergence creating new oceanic crust at the rate of 2 to 10 centimeters per year. Convergence is when the oceanic crust collides with either another oceanic plate or a continental plate. The oceanic crust sinks forming an enormous trench and generating volcanic activity. Convergence also includes continent to continent plate collisions. When two plates slide past one another a transform fault is created. These movements produce many major features of the earth's surface, such as mountain ranges, volcanoes, and earthquake zones. Most of these features are located at plate boundaries, where the plates interact by spreading apart, pressing together, or sliding past each other. These movements are very slow, averaging only a few centimeters a year.

Boundaries form between spreading plates where the crust is forced apart in a process called rifting. Rifting generally occurs at mid-ocean ridges. Rifting can also take place within a continent, splitting the continent into smaller, landmasses that drift away from each other, thereby forming an ocean basin (Red Sea) between them. As the seafloor spreading takes place, new material is added to the inner edges of the separating plates. In this way, the plates grow larger, and the ocean basin widens. This is the process that broke up the super continent Pangaea and created the Atlantic Ocean.

Boundaries between plates that are colliding are zones of intense crustal activity. When a plate of ocean crust collides with a plate of continental crust, the more dense oceanic plate slides under the lighter continental plate and plunges into the mantle. This process is called subduction, and the site where it takes place is called a subduction zone. A subduction zone is usually seen on the seafloor as a deep depression called a trench. The crustal movement which is characterized by plates sliding sideways past each other produces a plate boundary characterized by major faults that are capable of unleashing powerful earthquakes. The San Andreas Fault forms such a boundary between the Pacific Plate and the North American Plate.

Orogeny is the term given to natural mountain building. A mountain is terrain that has been raised high above the surrounding landscape by volcanic action, or some form of tectonic plate collisions. The plate collisions could be intercontinental or ocean floor collisions with a continental crust (subduction). The physical composition of mountains would include igneous, metamorphic, or sedimentary rocks; some may have rock layers that are tilted or distorted by plate collision forces.

There are many different types of mountains. The physical attributes of a mountain range depends upon the angle at which plate movement thrust layers of rock to the surface. Many mountains (Adirondacks, Southern Rockies) were formed along high angle faults. Folded mountains (Alps, Himalayas) are produced by the folding of rock layers during their formation. The Himalayas are the highest mountains in the world and contains Mount Everest which rises almost 9 km above sea level. The Himalayas were formed when India collided with Asia. The movement which created this collision is still in process at the rate of a few centimeters per year. Fault-block mountains (Utah, Arizona, and New Mexico) are created when plate movement produces tension forces instead of compression forces. The area under tension produces normal faults and rock along these faults is displaced upward. Dome mountains are formed as magma tries to push up through the crust but fails to break the surface. Dome mountains resemble a huge blister on the earth's surface. Upwarped mountains (Black Hills of S.D.) are created in association with a broad arching of the crust. They can also be formed by rock thrust upward along high angle faults.

Volcanic mountains are built up by successive deposits of volcanic materials. Volcanism is the term given to the movement of magma through the crust and its emergence as lava onto the earth's surface. An active volcano is one that is presently erupting or building to an eruption. A dormant volcano is one that is between eruptions but still shows signs of internal activity that might lead to an eruption in the future. An extinct volcano is said to be no longer capable of erupting. Most of the world's active volcanoes are found along the rim of the Pacific Ocean, which is also a major earthquake zone. This curving belt of active faults and volcanoes is often called the Ring of Fire. The world's best known volcanic mountains are Mount Etna in Italy and Mount Kilimanjaro in Africa. The Hawaiian Islands are actually the tops of a chain of volcanic mountains that rise from the ocean floor.

There are three types of volcanic mountains: shield volcanoes, cinder cones and composite volcanoes. Shield Volcanoes are associated with quiet eruptions. Lava emerges from the vent or opening in the crater and flows freely out over the earth's surface until it cools and hardens into a layer of igneous rock. A repeated lava flow builds this type of volcano into the largest volcanic mountain. Mauna Loa found in Hawaii, is the largest volcano on earth. Cinder Cone Volcanoes associated with explosive eruptions as lava is hurled high into the air in a spray of droplets of various sizes. These droplets cool and harden into cinders and particles of ash before falling to the ground. The ash and cinder pile up around the vent to form a steep, cone-shaped hill called the cinder cone. Cinder cone volcanoes are relatively small but may form quite rapidly. Composite Volcanoes are described as being built by both lava flows and layers of ash and cinders. Mount Fuji in Japan, Mount St. Helens in Washington, USA, and Mount Vesuvius in Italy are all famous Composite Volcanoes.

Glaciation

About 12,000 years ago, a vast sheet of ice covered a large part of the northern United States. This huge, frozen mass had moved southward from the northern regions of Canada as several large bodies of slow-moving ice, or glaciers. A time period in which glaciers advance over a large portion of a continent is called an ice age. A glacier is a large mass of ice that moves or flows over the land in response to gravity. Glaciers form among high mountains and in other cold regions. There are two main types of glaciers: valley glaciers and continental glaciers. Erosion by valley glaciers is characteristic of U-shaped erosion. They produce sharp peaked mountains such as the Matterhorn in Switzerland. Erosion by continental glaciers often rides over mountains in their paths leaving smoothed, rounded mountains and ridges. Evidence of the North American glacial coverage includes: abrasive grooves, large boulders from northern environments dropped in southerly locations, glacial troughs created by the rounding out of steep valleys by glacial scouring, and the remains of glacial sources that were created by frost wedging the rock at the bottom of the glacier (called cirques). Remains of plants and animals found in warm climates have been discovered in the moraines and out wash plains help to support the theory of periods of warmth during the past ice ages.

Skill 17.4   Interpret maps commonly used in earth science (e.g., topographic maps, globes, map projections)

A system of imaginary lines has been developed that helps people describe exact locations on Earth. Looking at a globe of Earth, you will see lines drawn on it. The equator is drawn around Earth halfway between the North and South Poles. Latitude is a term used to describe distance in degrees north or south of the equator. Lines of latitude are drawn east and west, parallel to the equator. Degrees of latitude range from 0 at the equator to 90 at either the North Pole or South Pole. Lines of latitude are also called parallels. Lines drawn north and south at right angles to the equator and from pole to pole are called meridians. Longitude is a term used to describe distances in degrees east or west of a meridian. The prime meridian passes through Greenwich, England.

Time zones are determined by longitudinal lines. Each time zone represents one hour. Since there are 24 hours in one complete rotation of the Earth, there are 24 international time zones. Each time zone is roughly 15 degrees wide. While time zones are based on meridians, they do not strictly follow lines of longitude. Time zone boundaries are subject to political decisions and have been moved around cities and other areas at the whim of the electorate.

The International Date Line is the 180 degree meridian and it is on the opposite side of the world from the prime meridian. The International Date Line is one-half of one day or 12 time zones from the prime meridian. If you were traveling west across the International Date Line, you would lose one day. If you were traveling east across the International Date Line, you would gain one day.

Principles of contouring

A contour line is a line on a map representing an imaginary line on the ground that has the same elevation above sea level along its entire length. Contour intervals usually are given in even numbers or as a multiple of five. In mapping mountains, a large contour interval is used. Small contour intervals may be used where there are small differences in elevation. Relief describes how much variation in elevation an area has. Rugged or high relief, describes an area of many hills and valleys. Gentle or low relief describes a plain area or a coastal region. Five general rules should be remembered in studying contour lines on a map.

1. Contour lines close around hills and basins or depressions. Hachure lines are used to show depressions. Hachures are short lines placed at right angles to the contour line and they always point toward the lower elevation.
2. Contours lines never cross. Contour lines are sometimes very close together. Each contour line represents a certain height above sea level.
3. Contour lines appear on both sides of an area where the slope reverses direction. Contour lines show where an imaginary horizontal plane would slice through a hillside or cut both sides of a valley.
4. Contours lines form V's that point upstream when they cross streams. Streams cut beneath the general elevation of the land surface, and contour lines follow a valley.
5. All contours lines either close (connect) or extend to the edge of the map.
6. No map is large enough to have all its contour lines close.

Interpret maps and imagery

Like photographs, maps readily display information that would be impractical to express in words. Maps that show the shape of the land are called topographic maps. Topographic maps, which are also referred to as quadrangles, are generally classified according to publication scale. Relief refers to the difference in elevation between any two points. Maximum relief refers to the difference in elevation between the high test and lowest points in the area being considered. Relief determines the contour interval, which is the difference in elevation between succeeding contour lines that are used on topographic maps. Map scales express the relationship between distance or area on the map to the true distance or area on the earth's surface. It is expressed as so many feet, (miles, meters, km, or degrees) per inch (cm), of map.

Skill 17.5 Identify the ecological impact of geologic events (e.g., earthquakes, volcanic activity)

Natural phenomena affect the make up and functioning of ecosystems both directly and indirectly. For example, floods and volcanic eruptions can destroy the fixed portions of an ecosystem, such as plants and microbes. Mobile elements, such as animals, must evacuate or risk injury or death. After a catastrophic event, species of microbes and plants begin to repopulate the ecosystem, beginning a line of secondary succession that eventually leads to the return of higher-level species. Often the area affected by the event returns to something like its original state.

Volcanic eruptions produce large amounts of molten lava and expel large amounts of ash and gas. Molten lava kills and destroys any living organisms it contacts. However, when lava cools and hardens, it provides a rich environment for growth of microbes and plants. Volcanic eruptions also affect ecosystems indirectly. Studies show that the ash and gas released by eruptions can cause a reduction in the area temperature for several years. The volcanic aerosol reflects the Sun's rays and creates clouds that have the same effect. In addition, sulfuric acid released by the volcano suppresses the production of greenhouse gases that damage the ozone layer.

Floods destroy microbes and vegetation and kill or force the evacuation of animals. Only when floodwaters recede can an ecosystem begin to return to normal. Floods, however, also have indirect effects. For example, floods can cause permanent soil erosion and nutrient depletion. Such disruptions of the soil can delay and limit an ecosystem's recovery.

An earthquake is the shaking or displacement of the ground at the Earth's surface that results from a sudden release of stored energy in the crust that propagates seismic waves. Earthquakes generally occur along fault lines and are detected by seismometers. Earthquakes occur on a daily basis around the world and, in most cases, cause little to no damage. Large earthquakes, however, can cause severe property damage and loss of life through various agents of damage. These factors include fault rupture, vibratory ground motion, inundation, permanent ground failure, fire and release of hazardous materials. Historically, the most common and dominant agent of damage is vibratory ground motion (shaking) that is capable of disrupting all infrastructures such as buildings, roads, pipelines and power lines. Inundation describes numerous earthquake related phenomena such as tsunamis and dam failure. Earthquakes may cause tsunamis by rapid and massive vertical displacement in a body of water, such as an ocean.

Damage caused by an earthquake depends largely on the earthquake's magnitude and duration. These two factors are determined by the amount of stress that accumulates in the Earth's crust and the amount of energy released when this stress causes tectonic plates to slip.

COMPETENCY 18.0 UNDERSTAND WATER AND THE HYDROSPHERE

Skill 18.1 Identify characteristics of freshwater and saltwater (e.g., specific heat, density, salinity)

Seventy percent of the earth's surface is covered with saltwater which is termed the hydrosphere. The mass of this saltwater is about 1.4×10^{24} grams. The ocean waters continuously circulate among different parts of the hydrosphere. There are seven major oceans: the North Atlantic Ocean, South Atlantic Ocean, North Pacific Ocean, South Pacific Ocean, Indian Ocean, Arctic Ocean, and the Antarctic Ocean.

Pure water is a combination of hydrogen and oxygen. These two elements make up about 96.5% of the ocean water. The remaining portion is made up of dissolved solids. The concentration of these dissolved solids determines the water's salinity. Salinity is the number of grams of these dissolved salts in 1,000 grams of seawater. The average salinity of ocean water is about 3.5%. In other words, one kilogram of seawater contains about 35 grams of salt, also commonly stated as 35 ppt (parts per thousand). Sodium Chloride or salt (NaCl) is the most abundant of the dissolved salts. The dissolved salts also include smaller quantities of magnesium chloride, magnesium and calcium sulfates, and traces of several other salt elements. Salinity varies throughout the world's oceans; the total salinity of the oceans varies from place to place and also varies with depth. Salinity is low near river mouths where the ocean mixes with fresh water, and salinity is high in areas of high evaporation rates.

The temperature of ocean water varies with different latitudes and with ocean depths. Ocean water temperature is about constant to depths of 90 meters (m). The temperature of surface water will drop rapidly from 28° C at the equator to -2° C at the Poles. The freezing point of seawater is lower than the freezing point of pure water. Pure water freezes at 0° C. The dissolved salts in seawater keep the freezing point of seawater at -2° C. The freezing point of seawater may vary depending upon its salinity in a particular location.

The density of pure water is 1000 kg/m3. Ocean water is more dense because in contains salt. Density of ocean water at the sea surface is approximately 1027 kg/m3. Ocean water can be more dense than this figure if the conditions are changed. Ocean water is more dense as its temperature decreases (colder water = more dense). This is true for salinity as well; increasing the concentration of salt will increase the density of sea water. Less dense water almost always floats on top of more dense water. Given two layers of water with the same salinity, the warmer water will float on top of the colder water. The only exception would be if both temperature *and* salinity were variable.

A unique property of water is that its cooler, solid phase (ice) is less dense/lighter than the liquid phase. Hence ice floats and water freezes over. You may have noticed however, that lakes more readily freeze than oceans. This has to do with salinity and specific heat. Salt water requires a lower temperature (than pure water) to freeze. The specific heat of a substance is the amount of heat required to raise the temperature of 1 gram of the substance by 1°C. Because water molecules have special bonding properties (adhesion), it is hard to separate them. Therefore, a lot of energy is required and water has the highest specific heat of all materials.

Skill 18.2　Identify characteristics and effects of the water cycle (e.g., cloud formation, precipitation, transpiration)

Water that falls to Earth in the form of rain and snow is called precipitation. Precipitation is part of a continuous process in which water at the Earth's surface evaporates, condenses into clouds, and returns to Earth. This process is termed the water cycle. The water located below the surface is called groundwater.

The air temperature at which water vapor begins to condense is called the dew point. Relative humidity is the actual amount of water vapor in a certain volume of air compared to the maximum amount of water vapor this air could hold at a given temperature.

Condensation or the removal of water above the Earth's surface results in the formation of clouds. Generally, clouds develop in any air mass that becomes saturated or has a relative humidity of 100%. Certain processes that cool the temperature of an air mass to its dew point or frost point can cause saturation. There are four processes or any combination of these processes that create saturation and cause clouds to form:

1. Orographic uplift occurs when elevated land forces air to rise.
2. Convectional lifting is the result of surface heating of air at ground level. If enough heating occurs, the air rises, expands, and cools.
3. Convergence or frontal lifting occurs when two air masses come together. One of the air masses is usually warm and moist, while the other is cool and dry.
4. Radiative cooling usually occurs at night when the sun is no longer heating the ground and the surrounding air. The ground and the air begin to cool, forming fog.

Cloud types
    Cirrus clouds - White and feathery high in sky
    Cumulus - thick, white, fluffy
    Stratus - layers of clouds cover most of the sky
    Nimbus - heavy, dark clouds that represent thunderstorm clouds

Variations on the clouds mentioned above
    Cumulo-nimbus
    Strato-nimbus

An important part of the water cycle is transpiration. Transpiration is the evaporation of water into the atmosphere from plants. Plants absorb water through their roots. Plants have specialized tissue that carries the water and nutrients to its leaves. Evaporation of water occurs through small pores called stomata, which are found on the underside of the leaves. Transpiration accounts for approximately 10% of all evaporating water. When considering diversity and the interconnectedness of the Earth's processes, one should not forget transpiration. Trees who are many years old, as well as desert dwellers with adaptive long taproots, are able to acquire water from deep in the Earth, and bring it to the surface for all.

Skill 18.2   Recognize factors that affect the movement of surface water (e.g., tides, waves, riverbeds) and groundwater (e.g., soil characteristics, wells, water budgets)

Surface Water

World weather patterns are greatly influenced by ocean surface currents in the upper layer of the ocean. These currents continuously move along the ocean surface in specific directions. Ocean currents that flow deep below the surface are called sub-surface currents. These currents are influenced by such factors as the location of landmasses in the current's path and the earth's rotation.

Surface currents are caused by winds and are classified by temperature. Cold currents originate in the Polar regions and flow through surrounding water that is measurably warmer. Those currents with a higher temperature than the surrounding water are called warm currents and can be found near the equator. These currents follow swirling routes around the ocean basins and the equator. The Gulf Stream and the California Current are the two main surface currents that flow along the coastlines of the United States. The Gulf Stream is a warm current in the Atlantic Ocean that carries warm water from the equator to the northern parts of the Atlantic Ocean. Benjamin Franklin studied and named the Gulf Stream. The California Current is a cold current that originates in the Arctic regions and flows southward along the westcoast of the United States.

Differences in water density also create ocean currents. Water found near the bottom of oceans is the coldest and the densest. Water tends to flow from a denser area to a less dense area. Currents that flow because of a difference in the density of the ocean water are called density currents. Water with a higher salinity is denser than water with a lower salinity. Water that has salinity different from the surrounding water may form a density current.

The movement of ocean water is caused by the wind, the sun's heat energy, the earth's rotation, the moon's gravitational pull on earth, and by underwater earthquakes. Most ocean waves are caused by the impact of winds. Wind blowing over the surface of the ocean transfers energy (friction) to the water and causes waves to form. Waves are also formed by seismic activity on the ocean floor. A wave formed by an earthquake is called a seismic sea wave. These powerful waves can be very destructive, with wave heights increasing to 30 m or more near the shore. The crest of a wave is its highest point. The trough of a wave is its lowest point. The distance from wave top to wave top is the wavelength. The wave period is the time between the passings of two successive waves.

Rivers and streams are bodies of moving water. Characteristics of the river or stream change as it flows from its headwaters to the sea. Also, as the depth of stream/river increases, zones similar to those present in the ocean are seen. That is, different species live in the upper, sunlit areas (algae, top feeding fish, aquatic insects) and in the darker, bottom areas (catfish, carp, microbes). Rivers and streams are responsible for erosion and deposition.

Glaciers are rivers of ice that have formed over land. Glaciers are the largest stores of fresh water on Earth and are found on every continent, including on the greater Australian continent. Glaciers are considered long lasting, although recent studies have shown that their expanses are decreasing in response to global warming. As glaciers move they leave permanent indentations, called moraines and deep U-shaped valleys. The glacier fringe, where the glacier has melted into water, is a source of available water (as opposed to the unavailable water locked into the frozen glacier).

Ground Water

Water circulates through the environment via the water cycle. Two percent of all the Earth's available water is fixed and unavailable in ice or the bodies of organisms. Available water includes surface water (lakes, ocean, and rivers) and ground water (aquifers, wells). 96% of all available water is from ground water. Water is recycled through the processes of evaporation and precipitation. Water that falls to Earth in the form of rain and snow is called **precipitation.** Precipitation is part of a continuous process in which water at the Earth's surface evaporates, condenses into clouds, and returns to Earth. The water located below the surface is called groundwater. The water present now is the water that has been here since our atmosphere formed.

Water flows and is collected in a predictable manner. In most situations, it runs across land and into small streams that feed larger bodies of water. All of the land that acts like a funnel for water flowing into a single larger body of water is known as a watershed or drainage basin. The watershed includes the streams and rivers that bear the water and the surfaces across which the water runs.

Thus, the pollution load and general state of all the land within a watershed has an effect on the health and cleanliness of the body of water to which it drains. Large land features, such as mountains, separate watersheds from one another. However, some portion of water from one watershed may enter the groundwater and ultimately flow towards another, adjacent watershed.

Not all water flows to the streams, rivers, and lakes that comprise the above ground water supply. Some water remains in the soil as ground water. Additionally, underground rivers are found in areas of karst topography, though these are relatively rare. It is more common for water to collect in underground aquifers. Aquifers are layers of permeable rock or loose material (gravel, sand, or silt) that hold water. Aquifers may be either confined or unconfined. Confined aquifers are deep in the ground and below the water table. Unconfined aquifers border on the water table. The water table is the level at which ground water exists and is always equal to atmospheric pressure. To visualize the entire ground water system, we can imagine a hole dug in wet sand at the beach and a small pool of water within the hole. The wet sand corresponds to the aquifer, the hole to a well or lake, and the level of water in the hole to the water table.

In some cases, people have created reservoirs, artificial storage areas that make large amounts of water readily available. Reservoirs are most often created by the damming of rivers. A dam is built from cement, soil, or rock and the river fills the newly created reservoir. A reservoir may be created by building a dam either across a valley or around the entire perimeter of an artificial lake (a bunded dam). The former technique is more common and relies on natural features to form a watertight reservoir. However, such a feature must exist to allow this type of construction. A fully bunded dam does not require such a natural feature but does necessitate more construction since a waterproof structure must be built all the way around the reservoir. This structure is typically made from clay and/or cement. Since no river feeds such reservoirs, mechanical pumps are used to fill them from nearby water sources. Occasionally, watertight roofs are added to these reservoirs so they can be used to hold treated water. These are known as service reservoirs.

Soils are composed of particles of sand, clay, various minerals, tiny living organisms, and humus, plus the decayed remains of plants and animals. Soil composition has an effect on water movement. Sandy soils are gritty and their particles do not bind together firmly. Sandy soils are porous; water passes through them rapidly. Therefore, sandy soils do not hold much water and therefore have poor **absorption.** Clay soils are smooth and greasy; their particles bind together firmly. Clay soils are moist and usually do not allow water to pass through easily. This type of soil has the lowest potential for **run off.** Loamy soils feel somewhat like velvet and their particles clump together. Loamy soils are made up of sand, clay, and silt. Loamy soils hold water but some water can pass through. **Percolation** is best in this type of soil.

Precipitation that soaks into the ground through small pores or openings becomes groundwater. Gravity causes groundwater to move through interconnected porous rock formations from higher to lower elevations. The upper surface of the zone saturated with groundwater is the water table. A swamp is an area where the water table is at the surface. Sometimes the land dips below the water table and these areas fill with water forming lakes, ponds or streams. Groundwater that flows out from underground onto the surface is called a spring.

Permeable rocks filled with water are called **aquifers**. When a layer of permeable rock is trapped between two layers of impermeable rock, an aquifer is formed. Groundwater fills the pore spaces in the permeable rock. Layers of limestone are common aquifers. Groundwater provides drinking water for 53% of the population in the United States and is collected in **reservoirs.**

Skill 18.3 Identify factors that affect the biological productivity of bodies of water

Biological productivity is a measure of the rate of growth and reproduction of the organisms in a given environment. It typically connotes an increase in biomass.

Biological productivity has several levels. Both terrestrial and aquatic food chains have photosynthetic (or occasionally, chemosynthetic) organisms at their base. The rate at which energy is stored by these photosynthetic organisms in the form of organic substances is known as basic or primary productivity. Plankton and algae occupy these low-level positions in ocean and freshwater environments, respectively. Heterotrophic organisms rely on the oxygen and complex sugars supplied by these phototrophs. One of the most important factors that determines primary productivity is the phototrophs' access to free nutrients such as nitrogen, phosphate, and silicone. Therefore, as the concentration of these nutrients increases in a given area, so does the primary biological productivity of that area. This means that certain pollutants, such as nitrogen-based fertilizer and phosphate containing detergents, may actually increase the primary productivity of aquatic environments, often leading to overgrowth. Because these organisms are photosynthetic, access to sunlight is also important. Thus, productivity is higher in locations that receive more hours of sunlight per day. In the oceans and large lakes, shore areas tend to have higher productivity per volume of water. This is because they are shallow and do not possess large amounts the deep, dark water common in the middle of oceans and lakes.

Additionally, there are secondary productivities, which correspond to productivity at the higher trophic levels (i.e., herbivore and carnivores higher up the food chain). As is logical, secondary productivity largely depends on primary productivity. If primary productivity decreases, secondary productivity will decrease. However, other factors can interrupt the food web and lower the secondary productivities even when primary productivity is high. For example, oxygen levels are naturally low in deep ocean waters and may be reduced artificially in streams and lakes by thermal pollution. Since animals need this oxygen to live, productivity in these areas will be lower. Additionally, the loss of native species or the introduction of foreign, invasive species may cause a gap in the food chain. The loss of this food source lowers the productivity of the "higher up" species that depend upon it. Furthermore, the animals that occupy each specific ecosystem are well adapted to it and so changes in the temperature, water flow rates, or concentrations of specific nutrients may negatively affect these species. Note that the introduction of pollutants and the presence of man-made structures and vehicles may introduce changes such as these.

COMPETENCY 19.0 UNDERSTAND WEATHER, CLIMATE, AND THE EARTH'S ATMOSPHERE

Skill 19.1 Identify the structure, functions, and characteristics of the earth's atmosphere

Dry air is composed of three basic components; dry gas, water vapor, and solid particles (dust from soil, etc.).

The most abundant dry gases in the atmosphere are:

(N_2)	Nitrogen	78.09 %	makes up about 4/5 of gases in atmosphere
(O_2)	Oxygen	20.95 %	
(AR)	Argon	0.93 %	
(CO_2)	Carbon Dioxide	0.03 %	

The atmosphere is divided into four main layers based on temperature. These layers are labeled Troposphere, Stratosphere, Mesosphere, Thermosphere.

Troposphere - this layer is the closest to the earth's surface and all weather phenomena occurs here as it is the layer with the most water vapor and dust. Air temperature decreases with increasing altitude. The average thickness of the Troposphere is 7 miles (11 km).

Stratosphere - this layer contains very little water, clouds within this layer are extremely rare. The Ozone layer is located in the upper portions of the stratosphere. Air temperature is fairly constant but does increase somewhat with height due to the absorption of solar energy and ultra violet rays from the ozone layer.

Mesosphere - air temperature again decreases with height in this layer. It is the coldest layer with temperatures in the range of -100^0 C at the top.

Thermosphere - extends upward into space. Oxygen molecules in this layer absorb energy from the sun, causing temperatures to increase with height. The lower part of the thermosphere is called the Ionosphere. Here charged particles or ions and free electrons can be found. When gases in the Ionosphere are excited by solar radiation, the gases give off light and glow in the sky. These glowing lights are called the Aurora Borealis in the Northern Hemisphere and Aurora Australis in Southern Hemisphere. The upper portion of the Thermosphere is called the Exosphere. Gas molecules are very far apart in this layer. Layers of Exosphere are also known as the Van Allen Belts and are held together by earth's magnetic field.

MID. LEVEL SCIENCE

Skill 19.2 Analyze the role of air masses and their movements in affecting weather

AIR MASSES:

Air masses moving toward or away from the Earth's surface are called air currents. Air moving parallel to Earth's surface is called **wind**. Weather conditions are generated by winds and air currents carrying large amounts of heat and moisture from one part of the atmosphere to another. Wind speeds are measured by instruments called anemometers.

FRONTS:

Fronts are the leading edges of air masses which have different density (air temperature and/or humidity) than the area it is passing into. When a front passes over an area, the area often experiences changes in temperature, moisture, wind speed/direction, atmospheric pressure, and even precipitation. Cold fronts are often associated with low pressure systems and bring cold, dry air. Warm fronts often bring warm, moist air which may feel tropical. Fronts are guided by winds and travel from west to east. Fronts may be manipulated by mountains and large bodies of water.

UPPER-LEVEL WIND PATTERNS:

The wind belts in each hemisphere consist of convection cells that encircle Earth like belts. There are three major wind belts on Earth: (1) trade winds (2) prevailing westerlies, and (3) polar easterlies. Wind belt formation depends on the differences in air pressures that develop in the doldrums, the horse latitudes, and the polar regions. The Doldrums surround the equator. Within this belt heated air usually rises straight up into Earth's atmosphere. The Horse latitudes are regions of high barometric pressure with calm and light winds and the Polar regions contain cold dense air that sinks to the Earth's surface.

Skill 19.3 Recognize processes related to precipitation and cloud formation

Energy is transferred in Earth's atmosphere in three ways. Earth gets most of its energy from the sun in the form of waves. This transfer of energy by waves is termed **radiation**. The transfer of thermal energy through matter by actual contact of molecules is called **conduction**. For example, heated rocks and sandy beaches transfer heat to the surrounding air. The transfer of thermal energy due to air density differences is called **convection**. Convection currents circulate in a constant exchange of cold, dense air for less dense warm air.

Carbon Dioxide in the atmosphere absorbs energy from the sun. Carbon Dioxide also blocks the direct escape of energy from the Earth's surface. This process by which heat is trapped by gases, water vapor and other gases in the Earth's atmosphere is called the **Greenhouse Effect**.

Most of the Earth's water is found in the oceans and lakes. Through the **water cycle**, water evaporates into the atmosphere and condenses into clouds. Water then falls to the Earth in the form of precipitation, returning to the oceans and lakes on falling on land. Water on the land may return to the oceans and lakes as runoff or seep from the soil as groundwater.

CLOUD TYPES:

Cirrus clouds - White and feathery; high in the sky

Cumulus – thick, white, fluffy

Stratus – layers of clouds cover most of the sky

Nimbus – heavy, dark clouds that represent thunderstorm clouds

Variation on the clouds mentioned above.

Cumulo-nimbus

Strato-nimbus

The air temperature at which water vapor begins to condense is called the **dew point.**

Relative humidity is the actual amount of water vapor in a certain volume of air compared to the maximum amount of water vapor this air could hold at a given temperature.

FORMATION:

Condensation or the removal of water above the Earth's surface results in the formation of clouds. Generally, clouds develop in any air mass that becomes saturated or has a relative humidity of 100%. Certain processes that cool the temperature of an air mass to its dew point or frost point can cause saturation. There are four processes or any combination of these processes that create saturation and cause clouds to form:

1. Orographic uplift occurs when elevated land forces air to rise.
2. Convectional lifting is the result of surface heating of air at ground level. If enough heating occurs, the air rises, expands, and cools.
3. Convergence or frontal lifting occurs when two air masses come together. One of the air masses is usually warm and moist, while the other is cool and dry.
4. Radiative cooling usually occurs at night when the sun is no longer heating the ground and the surrounding air. The ground and the air begin to cool, forming fog.

Skill 19.4   Analyze the use of maps, equipment, and techniques in predicting and interpreting weather and climatic changes

Every day every one of us is affected by weather regardless if it is the typical thunderstorm with the brief moist air coming down on us from a cumulonimbus cloud or a severe storm with pounding winds that can have wind factors that can cause either hurricanes or twisters called tornados. These are common terms that we can identify with including the term blizzards or ice storms.

The daily newscast relates terms such as dew point and relative humidity and barometric pressure. Suddenly all too common terms become clouded with terms more frequently used by a meteorologist or someone that forecasts weather. Dew point is the air temperature at which water vapor begins to condense. Relative humidity is the actual amount of water vapor in a certain volume of air compared to the maximum amount of water vapor that this air could hold at a given temperature.

Weather instruments that forecast weather include aneroid barometer and the mercury barometer that measures air pressure. The air exerts varying pressures on a metal diaphragm that will read air pressure. The mercury barometer operates when atmospheric pressure pushes on a pool of (mercury) in a glass tube. The higher the pressure, the higher up the tube the mercury rises.

Relative humidity is measured by two kinds of weather instruments, the psychrometer and the hair gygrometer. Relative humidity simply indicates the amount of moisture in the air. Relative humidity is defined as a ration of existing amounts of water vapor and moisture in the air when compared to the maximum amount of moisture that the air can hold at the same given pressure and temperature. Relative humidity is stated as a percentage so for example the relative humidity can be 100%.

For example if you were to analyze relative humidity from data, an example might be If a parcel of air is saturated, meaning it now holds all the moisture it can hold at a given temperature, the relative humidity is 100%.

Lesson Plans for teachers to analyze data and predict weather

http://www.srh.weather.gov/srh/jetstream/synoptic/ll_analyze.html

Skill 19.5 Identify the effects of weather events and climatic changes on ecosystems

The various biomes are characterized not only by the soil types and organisms present in them, but by their unique weather patterns. Indeed, the climate largely determines what organisms evolved to populate each of these ecosystems. Along with temperature profiles, precipitation patterns are the key component of the climate of an ecosystem. One of the most dramatic examples of a weather event's importance to an ecosystem is the annual rainfall on some arid grasslands and deserts. Though the plants and animals that live in these grasslands are adapted to dry conditions, they rely on the yearly rains to maintain their life cycles. Similarly, many ecosystems experience regular seasonal changes that provide cues to the organisms therein. The seasonal changes in temperature and precipitation may trigger the plants to sprout, drop seed pods, or become dormant and similarly signal animals to breed, eat more or less food, or enter hibernation. Even seemingly catastrophic events such as fire or flood are often part of the normal cycle of life in some ecosystems. Certain species have evolved mechanisms that allow them to survive these events, while for others, it is a time of renewal that removes old individuals and triggers growth of a new generation. This recovery is part of the natural phenomenon of succession, which is a normal and necessary process.

It should be clear then, that changes in climate would have significant effects on the species within an ecosystem. Because each biome's organisms are uniquely adapted to the conditions of that biome, they typically will not fare well when climatic or other changes are introduced. Changes in precipitation, annual temperature profiles, or availability of nutrients may shorten or even eliminate the growing season of an area. This, in turn, creates less food for the heterotrophic animals and may cause the death of organisms. Additionally, climatic changes may cause the loss of aquatic or arboreal habitats, thus endangering the species that rely upon them. Finally, if significant enough temperature changes are introduced, certain species may be unable to maintain their metabolism at the new temperature. Of course, some organisms will be able to survive in new conditions and even adapt to thrive. This is another type of succession; some species are lost, new organisms become prominent, and new relationships between the components of the food web are formed.

COMPETENCY 20.0 UNDERSTAND BASIC ASTRONOMY

Skill 20.1 Analyze theories of the structure, origin, and evolution of the solar system and universe

Two main hypotheses of the origin of the solar system are the **tidal hypothesis** and the **condensation hypothesis**.

The tidal hypothesis proposes that the solar system began with a near collision of the sun and a large star. Some astronomers believe that as these two stars passed each other, the great gravitational pull of the large star extracted hot gases out of the sun. The mass from the hot gases started to orbit the sun, which began to cool then condensing into the nine planets. (Few astronomers support this example).

The condensation hypothesis proposes that the solar system began with rotating clouds of dust and gas. Condensation occurred in the center forming the sun and the smaller parts of the cloud formed the nine planets. (This example is widely accepted by many astronomers).

Two main theories to explain the origins of the universe include the **Big Bang Theory** and the **Steady-State Theory.**

The Big Bang Theory has been widely accepted by many astronomers. It states that the universe originated from a magnificent explosion spreading mass, matter and energy into space. The galaxies formed from this material as it cooled during the next half-billion years.

The Steady-State Theory is the least accepted theory. It states that the universe is a continuously being renewed. Galaxies move outward and new galaxies replace the older galaxies. Astronomers have not found any evidence to prove this theory.

The future of the universe is hypothesized with the Oscillating Universe Hypothesis. It states that the universe will oscillate or expand and contract. Galaxies will move away from one another and will in time slow down and stop. Then a gradual moving toward each other will again activate the explosion or The Big Bang theory.

Skill 20.2 Identify the components of the solar system (e.g., sun, planets, moons, asteroids) and their characteristics, interactions, and movements

The **sun** is considered the nearest star to earth that produces solar energy. By the process of nuclear fusion, hydrogen gas is converted to helium gas. Energy flows out of the core to the surface, then radiation escapes into space.

Parts of the sun include: (1) **core**: the inner portion of the sun where fusion takes place, (2) **photosphere**: considered the surface of the sun which produces **sunspots** (cool, dark areas that can be seen on its surface), (3) **chromosphere**: hydrogen gas causes this portion to be red in color (also found here are solar flares (sudden brightness of the chromosphere) and solar prominences (gases that shoot outward from the chromosphere)), and (4) **corona**, the transparent area of sun visible only during a total eclipse.

PLANETS:

There are eight established planets in our solar system; Mercury, Venus, Earth, Mars, Jupiter, Saturn, Uranus, and Neptune. Pluto was an established planet in our solar system, but as of Summer 2006, its status is being reconsidered. The planets are divided into two groups based on distance from the sun. The inner planets include: Mercury, Venus, Earth, and Mars. The outer planets include: Jupiter, Saturn, Uranus, and Neptune.

Planets

Mercury -- the closest planet to the sun. Its surface has craters and rocks. The atmosphere is composed of hydrogen, helium and sodium. Mercury was named after the Roman messenger god.

Venus - has a slow rotation when compared to Earth. Venus and Uranus rotate in opposite directions from the other planets. This opposite rotation is called retrograde rotation. The surface of Venus is not visible due to the extensive cloud cover. The atmosphere is composed mostly of carbon dioxide. Sulfuric acid droplets in the dense cloud cover give Venus a yellow appearance. Venus has a greater greenhouse effect than observed on Earth. The dense clouds combined with carbon dioxide trap heat. Venus was named after the Roman goddess of love.

Earth - considered a water planet with 70% of its surface covered by water. Gravity holds the masses of water in place. The different temperatures observed on earth allow for the different states (solid. liquid, gas) of water to exist. The atmosphere is composed mainly of oxygen and nitrogen. Earth is the only planet that is known to support life.

Mars - the surface of Mars contains numerous craters, active and extinct volcanoes, ridges, and valleys with extremely deep fractures. Iron oxide found in the dusty soil makes the surface seem rust colored and the skies seem pink in color. The atmosphere is composed of carbon dioxide, nitrogen, argon, oxygen and water vapor. Mars has polar regions with ice caps composed of water. Mars has two satellites. Mars was named after the Roman war god.

Jupiter - largest planet in the solar system. Jupiter has 16 moons. The atmosphere is composed of hydrogen, helium, methane and ammonia. There are white colored bands of clouds indicating rising gas and dark colored bands of clouds indicating descending gases. The gas movement is caused by heat resulting from the energy of Jupiter's core. Jupiter has a Great Red Spot that is thought to be a hurricane type cloud. Jupiter has a strong magnetic field.

Saturn - the second largest planet in the solar system. Saturn has rings of ice, rock, and dust particles circling it. Saturn's atmosphere is composed of hydrogen, helium, methane, and ammonia. Saturn has 20 plus satellites. Saturn was named after the Roman god of agriculture.

Uranus - the second largest planet in the solar system with retrograde revolution. Uranus is a gaseous planet. It has 10 dark rings and 15 satellites. Its atmosphere is composed of hydrogen, helium, and methane. Uranus was named after the Greek god of the heavens.

Neptune - another gaseous planet with an atmosphere consisting of hydrogen, helium, and methane. Neptune has 3 rings and 2 satellites. Neptune was named after the Roman sea god because its atmosphere is the same color as the seas.

Pluto - once considered the smallest planet in the solar system, it's status as a planet is being reconsidered. Pluto's atmosphere probably contains methane, ammonia, and frozen water. Pluto has 1 satellite. Pluto revolves around the sun every 250 years. Pluto was named after the Roman god of the underworld.

COMETS/ASTEROIDS:

Comets, asteroids, and meteors.
Astronomers believe that rocky fragments may have been the remains of the birth of the solar system that never formed into a planet. **Asteroids** are found in the region between Mars and Jupiter.

Comets are masses of frozen gases, cosmic dust, and small rocky particles. Astronomers think that most comets originate in a dense comet cloud beyond Pluto. Comet consists of a nucleus, a coma, and a tail. A comet's tail always points away from the sun. The most famous comet, **Halley's Comet,** is named after the person whom first discovered it in 240 B.C. It returns to the skies near earth every 75 to 76 years.

Meteoroids are composed of particles of rock and metal of various sizes. When a meteoroid travels through the earth's atmosphere, friction causes its surface to heat up and it begins to burn. The burning meteoroid falling through the earth's atmosphere is called a **meteor** (also known as a "shooting star").

Meteorites are meteors that strike the earth's surface. A physical example of a meteorite's impact on the earth's surface can be seen in Arizona. The Barringer Crater is a huge meteor crater. There are many other meteor craters throughout the world.

INTERACTIONS:

The mass of any celestial object may be determined by using Newton's laws of motion and his law of gravity. In our solar system, measurable objects range in mass from the largest, the Sun, to the smallest, a near-Earth asteroid. (This does not take into account objects with a mass less than 10^{21} kg.)

The surface temperature of an object depends largely upon its proximity to the Sun. One exception to this, however, is Venus, which is hotter than Mercury because of its cloud layer that holds heat to the planet's surface. The surface temperatures of the planets range from more than 400 degrees on Mercury and Venus to below -200 degrees on the distant planets.

Most minor bodies in the solar system do not have any atmosphere and, therefore, can easily radiate the heat from the Sun. In the case of any celestial object, whether a side is warm or cold depends upon whether it faces the sun or not and the time of rotation. The longer rotation takes, the colder the side facing away from the sun will become, and vice versa.

If the density of an object is less than 1.5 grams per cc, then the object is almost exclusively made of frozen water, ammonia, carbon dioxide, or methane. If the density is less than 1.0, the object must be made of mostly gas. In our solar system, there is only one object with that low a density - Saturn. If the density is greater than 3.0 grams per cc, then the object is almost exclusively made of rocks; and if the density exceeds 5.0 grams per cc, then there must be a nickel-iron core. Densities between 1.5 and 3.0 indicate a rocky-ice mixture.

The density of planets correlates with their distance from the Sun. The inner planets (Mercury-Mars) are known as the terrestrial planets because they are rocky, and the outer planets (Jupiter and outward) are known as the icy or Jovian (gaslike) planets.

In order for two bodies to interact gravitationally, they must have significant mass. When two bodies in the solar system interact gravitationally, they orbit about a fixed point (the center of mass of the two bodies). This point lies on an imaginary line between the bodies, joining them such that the distances to each body multiplied by each body's mass are equal. The orbits of these bodies will vary slightly over time because of the gravitational interactions. The gravitational pull of Earth's moon is responsible for our tides.

Skill 20.3   Identify the characteristics of stars and galaxies

STARS:

A star is a ball of hot, glowing gas that is hot enough and dense enough to trigger nuclear reactions, which fuel the star. In comparing the mass, light production, and size of the Sun to other stars, astronomers find that the Sun is a perfectly ordinary star. It behaves exactly the way they would expect a star of its size to behave. The main difference between the Sun and other stars is that the Sun is much closer to Earth.

Most stars have masses similar to that of the Sun. The majority of stars' masses are between 0.3 to 3.0 times the mass of the Sun. Theoretical calculations indicate that in order to trigger nuclear reactions and to create its own energy—that is, to become a star—a body must have a mass greater than 7 percent of the mass of the Sun. Astronomical bodies that are less massive than this become planets or objects called brown dwarfs. The largest accurately determined stellar mass is of a star called V382 Cygni and is 27 times that of the Sun.

The range of brightness among stars is much larger than the range of mass. Astronomers measure the brightness of a star by measuring its magnitude and luminosity. Magnitude allows astronomers to rank how bright, comparatively, different stars appear to humans. Because of the way our eyes detect light, a lamp ten times more luminous than a second lamp will appear less than ten times brighter to human eyes. This discrepancy affects the magnitude scale, as does the tradition of giving brighter stars lower magnitudes. The lower a star's magnitude, the brighter it is. Stars with negative magnitudes are the brightest of all.

Magnitude is given in terms of absolute and apparent values. Absolute magnitude is a measurement of how bright a star would appear if viewed from a set distance away. Astronomers also measure a star's brightness in terms of its luminosity. A star's absolute luminosity or intrinsic brightness is the total amount of energy radiated by the star per second. Luminosity is often expressed in units of watts.

Astronomers use groups or patterns of stars called **constellations** as reference points to locate other stars in the sky. Familiar constellations include: Ursa Major (also known as the big bear) and Ursa Minor (known as the little bear). Within the Ursa Major, the smaller constellation, The Big Dipper is found. Within the Ursa Minor, the smaller constellation, The Little Dipper is found.

Different constellations appear as the earth continues its revolution around the sun with the seasonal changes. Magnitude stars are 21 of the brightest stars that can be seen from earth. These are the first stars noticed at night. In the Northern Hemisphere there are 15 commonly observed first magnitude stars.

GALAXIES:

Vast collections of stars are defined as **galaxies**. Galaxies are classified as irregular, elliptical, and spiral. An irregular galaxy has no real structured appearance; most are in their early stages of life. An elliptical galaxy consists of smooth ellipses, containing little dust and gas, but composed of millions or trillion stars. Spiral galaxies are disk-shaped and have extending arms that rotate around its dense center. Earth's galaxy is found in the Milky Way and it is a spiral galaxy.

Terms related to deep space

A **pulsar** is defined as a variable radio source that emits signals in very short, regular bursts; believed to be a rotating neutron star.

A **quasar** is defined as an object that photographs like a star but has an extremely large redshift and a variable energy output; believed to be the active core of a very distant galaxy.

Black holes are defined as an object that has collapsed to such a degree that light can not escape from its surface; light is trapped by the intense gravitational field.

Nebulae are clouds of dust and gas. These clouds are the birth place for stars. Nebulae are formed either because of a nearby supernova explosion or because a star has died, expelling some of its outermost content.

Skill 20.4   Recognize the significance and advancement of space exploration and its impact on society

Space exploration, like all scientific endeavors, provides the expansion of our knowledge about how the universe works. However, given the relatively high cost of space exploration, further justification is needed. Firstly, money spent on space research creates many jobs and so has economic benefits. Secondly, as space exploration has become an increasingly international affair, it has served to increase cooperation between nations and generate goodwill. Note that such cooperation also decreases the financial burden for individual countries. However, one of the greatest benefits of space exploration is the potential for transfer of technology. A vast array of technologies developed to further space exploration has found broader applications. These include communication devices, satellite operations, electronics, fabrics, and other materials. For instance, the technology used in smoke detectors was developed for NASA's Skylab spacecraft in the 1970s and quartz timing crystals used in nearly all wristwatches were developed as timing devices for the Apollo lunar missions.

Sample Test

Directions: Read each item and select the correct response.

1. In an experiment, the scientist states that he believes a change in the color of a liquid is due to a change of pH. This is an example of _____ .

A. observing.

B. inferring.

C. measuring.

D. classifying.

2. When is a hypothesis formed?

A. Before the data is taken.

B. After the data is taken.

C. After the data is analyzed.

D. Concurrent with graphing the data.

3. Who determines the laws regarding the use of safety glasses in the classroom?

A. The state.

B. The school site.

C. The Federal government.

D. The district level.

4. If one inch equals 2.54 cm how many mm in 1.5 feet? (APPROXIMATELY)

A. 18 mm.

B. 1800 mm.

C. 460 mm.

D. 4,600 mm.

5. Which of the following instruments measures wind speed?

A. A barometer.

B. An anemometer.

C. A wind sock.

D. A weather vane.

6. Sonar works by _____ .

A. Timing how long it takes sound to reach a certain speed.

B. Bouncing sound waves between two metal plates.

C. Bouncing sound waves off an underwater object and timing how long it takes for the sound to return.

D. Evaluating the motion and amplitude of sound.

7. The measure of the pull of the earth's gravity on an object is called _____ .

A. mass number.

B. atomic number.

C. mass.

D. weight.

8. Which reaction below is a decomposition reaction?

A. HCl + NaOH → NaCl + H_2O

B. C + O_2 → CO_2

C. $2H_2O$ → $2H_2$ + O_2

D. $CuSO_4$ + Fe → $FeSO_4$ + Cu

9. The Law of Conservation of Energy states that _____ .

A. There must be the same number of products and reactants in any chemical equation.

B. Objects always fall toward large masses such as planets.

C. Energy is neither created nor destroyed, but may change form.

D. Lights must be turned off when not in use, by state regulation.

10. Which parts of an atom are located inside the nucleus?

A. electrons and neutrons.

B. protons and neutrons.

C. protons only.

D. neutrons only.

11. The elements in the modern Periodic Table are arranged _____ .

A. in numerical order by atomic number.

B. randomly.

C. in alphabetical order by chemical symbol.

D. in numerical order by atomic mass.

12. Carbon bonds with hydrogen by _____ .

A. ionic bonding.

B. non-polar covalent bonding.

C. polar covalent bonding.

D. strong nuclear force.

13. Vinegar is an example of a _____.

A. strong acid.

B. strong base.

C. weak acid.

D. weak base.

14. Which of the following is not a nucleotide?

A. adenine.

B. alanine.

C. cytosine.

D. guanine.

15. When measuring the volume of water in a graduated cylinder, where does one read the measurement?

A. At the highest point of the liquid.

B. At the bottom of the meniscus curve.

C. At the closest mark to the top of the liquid.

D. At the top of the plastic safety ring.

16. A duck's webbed feet are examples of _____.

A. mimicry.

B. structural adaptation.

C. protective resemblance.

D. protective coloration.

17. What cell organelle contains the cell's stored food?

A. Vacuoles.

B. Golgi Apparatus.

C. Ribosomes.

D. Lysosomes.

18. The first stage of mitosis is called _____.

A. telophase.

B. anaphase.

C. prophase.

D. mitophase.

19. The Doppler Effect is associated most closely with which property of waves?

A. amplitude.

B. wavelength.

C. frequency.

D. intensity.

20. Viruses are responsible for many human diseases including all of the following except _____ ?

A. influenza.

B. A.I.D.S.

C. the common cold.

D. strep throat.

21. A series of experiments on pea plants formed by _____ showed that two invisible markers existed for each trait, and one marker dominated the other.

A. Pasteur.

B. Watson and Crick.

C. Mendel.

D. Mendeleev.

22. Formaldehyde should not be used in school laboratories for the following reason:

A. it smells unpleasant.

B. it is a known carcinogen.

C. it is expensive to obtain.

D. it is explosive.

23. Amino acids are carried to the ribosome in protein synthesis by _____ .

A. transfer RNA (tRNA).

B. messenger RNA (mRNA).

C. ribosomal RNA (rRNA).

D. transformation RNA (trRNA).

24. When designing a scientific experiment, a student considers all the factors that may influence the results. The process goal is to _____.

A. recognize and manipulate independent variables.

B. recognize and record independent variables.

C. recognize and manipulate dependent variables.

D. recognize and record dependent variables.

25. Since ancient times, people have been entranced with bird flight. What is the key to bird flight?

A. Bird wings are a particular shape and composition.

B. Birds flap their wings quickly enough to propel themselves.

C. Birds take advantage of tailwinds.

D. Birds take advantage of crosswinds.

26. Laboratory researchers have classified fungi as distinct from plants because the cell walls of fungi _____ .

A. contain chitin.

B. contain yeast.

C. are more solid.

D. are less solid.

27. In a fission reactor, "heavy water" is used to _____ .

A. terminate fission reactions.

B. slow down neutrons and moderate reactions.

C. rehydrate the chemicals.

D. initiate a chain reaction.

28. The transfer of heat by electromagnetic waves is called _____ .

A. conduction.

B. convection.

C. phase change.

D. radiation.

29. When heat is added to most solids, they expand. Why is this the case?

A. The molecules get bigger.

B. The faster molecular motion leads to greater distance between the molecules.

C. The molecules develop greater repelling electric forces.

D. The molecules form a more rigid structure.

30. The force of gravity on earth causes all bodies in free fall to _____ .

A. fall at the same speed.

B. accelerate at the same rate.

C. reach the same terminal velocity.

D. move in the same direction.

31. Sound waves are produced by _____ .

A. pitch.

B. noise.

C. vibrations.

D. sonar.

32. Resistance is measured in units called _____ .

A. watts.

B. volts.

C. ohms.

D. current.

33. Sound can be transmitted in all of the following *except* _____ .

A. air.

B. water.

C. a diamond.

D. a vacuum.

34. As a train approaches, the whistle sounds _____ .

A. higher, because it has a higher apparent frequency.

B. lower, because it has a lower apparent frequency.

C. higher, because it has a lower apparent frequency.

D. lower, because it has a higher apparent frequency.

35. The speed of light is different in different materials. This is responsible for _____ .

A. interference.

B. refraction.

C. reflection.

D. relativity.

36. A converging lens produces a real image _____ .

A. always.

B. never.

C. when the object is within one focal length of the lens.

D. when the object is further than one focal length from the lens.

37. The electromagnetic radiation with the longest wave length is/are _____ .

A. radio waves.

B. red light.

C. X-rays.

D. ultraviolet light.

38. Under a 440 power microscope, an object with diameter 0.1 millimeter appears to have a diameter of _____ .

A. 4.4 millimeters.

B. 44 millimeters.

C. 440 millimeters.

D. 4400 millimeters.

39. Separating blood into blood cells and plasma involves the process of _____ .

A. electrophoresis.

B. spectrophotometry.

C. centrifugation.

D. chromatography.

40. Experiments may be done with any of the following animals except _____ .

A. birds.

B. invertebrates.

C. lower order life.

D. frogs.

41. For her first project of the year, a student is designing a science experiment to test the effects of light and water on plant growth. You should recommend that she _____.

A. manipulate the temperature also.

B. manipulate the water pH also.

C. determine the relationship between light and water unrelated to plant growth.

D. omit either water or light as a variable.

42. In a laboratory report, what is the abstract?

A. The abstract is a summary of the report, and is the first section of the report.

B. The abstract is a summary of the report, and is the last section of the report.

C. The abstract is predictions for future experiments, and is the first section of the report.

D. The abstract is predictions for future experiments, and is the last section of the report.

43. What is the scientific method?

A. It is the process of doing an experiment and writing a laboratory report.

B. It is the process of using open inquiry and repeatable results to establish theories.

C. It is the process of reinforcing scientific principles by confirming results.

D. It is the process of recording data and observations.

44. Identify the control in the following experiment: A student had four corn plants and was measuring photosynthetic rate (by measuring growth mass). Half of the plants were exposed to full (constant) sunlight, and the other half were kept in 50% (constant) sunlight.

A. The control is a set of plants grown in full (constant) sunlight.

B. The control is a set of plants grown in 50% (constant) sunlight.

C. The control is a set of plants grown in the dark.

D. The control is a set of plants grown in a mixture of natural levels of sunlight.

45. In an experiment measuring the growth of bacteria at different temperatures, what is the independent variable?

A. Number of bacteria.

B. Growth rate of bacteria.

C. Temperature.

D. Light intensity.

46. A scientific law _____.

A. proves scientific accuracy.

B. may never be broken.

C. may be revised in light of new data.

D. is the result of one excellent experiment.

47. Which is the correct order of methodology?

1. collecting data
2. planning a controlled experiment
3. drawing a conclusion
4. hypothesizing a result
5. re-visiting a hypothesis to answer a question

A. 1,2,3,4,5

B. 4,2,1,3,5

C. 4,5,1,3,2

D. 1,3,4,5,2

48. Which is the most desirable tool to use to heat substances in a middle school laboratory?

A. Alcohol burner.

B. Freestanding gas burner.

C. Bunsen burner.

D. Hot plate.

49. Newton's Laws are taught in science classes because _____ .

A. they are the correct analysis of inertia, gravity, and forces.

B. they are a close approximation to correct physics, for usual Earth conditions.

C. they accurately incorporate relativity into studies of forces.

D. Newton was a well-respected scientist in his time.

50. Which of the following is most accurate?

A. Mass is always constant; Weight may vary by location.

B. Mass and Weight are both always constant.

C. Weight is always constant; Mass may vary by location.

D. Mass and Weight may both vary by location.

51. Chemicals should be stored

A. in the principal's office.

B. in a dark room.

C. in an off-site research facility.

D. according to their reactivity with other substances.

52. Which of the following is the worst choice for a school laboratory activity?

A. A genetics experiment tracking the fur color of mice.

B. Dissection of a preserved fetal pig.

C. Measurement of goldfish respiration rate at different temperatures.

D. Pithing a frog to watch the circulatory system.

53. Who should be notified in the case of a serious chemical spill?

A. The custodian.

B. The fire department or their municipal authority.

C. The science department chair.

D. The School Board.

54. A scientist exposes mice to cigarette smoke, and notes that their lungs develop tumors. Mice that were not exposed to the smoke do not develop as many tumors. Which of the following conclusions may be drawn from these results?

I. Cigarette smoke causes lung tumors.

II. Cigarette smoke exposure has a positive correlation with lung tumors in mice.

III. Some mice are predisposed to develop lung tumors.

IV. Mice are often a good model for humans in scientific research.

A. I and II only.

B. II only.

C. I, II, and III only.

D. II and IV only.

55. In which situation would a science teacher be legally liable?

A. The teacher leaves the classroom for a telephone call and a student slips and injures him/herself.

B. A student removes his/her goggles and gets acid in his/her eye.

C. A faulty gas line in the classroom causes a fire.

D. A student cuts him/herself with a dissection scalpel.

56. Which of these is the best example of 'negligence'?

A. A teacher fails to give oral instructions to those with reading disabilities.

B. A teacher fails to exercise ordinary care to ensure safety in the classroom.

C. A teacher displays inability to supervise a large group of students.

D. A teacher reasonably anticipates that an event may occur, and plans accordingly.

57. Which item should always be used when handling glassware?

A. Tongs.

B. Safety goggles.

C. Gloves.

D. Buret stand.

58. Which of the following is *not* a necessary characteristic of living things?

A. Movement.

B. Reduction of local entropy.

C. Ability to cause change in local energy form.

D. Reproduction.

59. What are the most significant and prevalent elements in the biosphere?

A. Carbon, Hydrogen, Oxygen, Nitrogen, Phosphorus.

B. Carbon, Hydrogen, Sodium, Iron, Calcium.

C. Carbon, Oxygen, Sulfur, Manganese, Iron.

D. Carbon, Hydrogen, Oxygen, Nickel, Sodium, Nitrogen.

60. All of the following measure energy *except* for _____

A. joules.

B. calories.

C. watts.

D. ergs.

61. Identify the correct sequence of organization of living things from lower to higher order:

A. Cell, Organelle, Organ, Tissue, System, Organism.

B. Cell, Tissue, Organ, Organelle, System, Organism.

C. Organelle, Cell, Tissue, Organ, System, Organism.

D. Organelle, Tissue, Cell, Organ, System, Organism.

62. Which kingdom is comprised of organisms made of one cell with no nuclear membrane?

A. Monera.

B. Protista.

C. Fungi.

D. Algae.

63. Which of the following is found in the least abundance in organic molecules?

A. Phosphorus.

B. Potassium.

C. Carbon.

D. Oxygen.

64. Catalysts assist reactions by _____ .

A. lowering effective activation energy.

B. maintaining precise pH levels.

C. keeping systems at equilibrium.

D. adjusting reaction speed.

65. Accepted procedures for preparing solutions should be made with _____ .

A. alcohol.

B. hydrochloric acid.

C. distilled water.

D. tap water.

66. Enzymes speed up reactions by _____ .

A. utilizing ATP.

B. lowering pH, allowing reaction speed to increase.

C. increasing volume of substrate.

D. lowering energy of activation.

67. When you step out of the shower, the floor feels colder on your feet than the bathmat. Which of the following is the correct explanation for this phenomenon?

A. The floor is colder than the bathmat.

B. Your feet have a chemical reaction with the floor, but not the bathmat.

C. Heat is conducted more easily into the floor.

D. Water is absorbed from your feet into the bathmat.

68. Which of the following is *not* considered ethical behavior for a scientist?

A. Using unpublished data and citing the source.

B. Publishing data before other scientists have had a chance to replicate results.

C. Collaborating with other scientists from different laboratories.

D. Publishing work with an incomplete list of citations.

69. The chemical equation for water formation is: $2H_2 + O_2 \rightarrow 2H_2O$. Which of the following is an *incorrect* interpretation of this equation?

A. Two moles of hydrogen gas and one mole of oxygen gas combine to make two moles of water.

B. Two grams of hydrogen gas and one gram of oxygen gas combine to make two grams of water.

C. Two molecules of hydrogen gas and one molecule of oxygen gas combine to make two molecules of water.

D. Four atoms of hydrogen (combined as a diatomic gas) and two atoms of oxygen (combined as a diatomic gas) combine to make two molecules of water.

70. Energy is measured with the same units as _____.

A. force.

B. momentum.

C. work.

D. power.

71. If the volume of a confined gas is increased, what happens to the pressure of the gas? You may assume that the gas behaves ideally, and that temperature and number of gas molecules remain constant.

A. The pressure increases.

B. The pressure decreases.

C. The pressure stays the same.

D. There is not enough information given to answer this question.

72. A product of anaerobic respiration in animals is _____.

A. carbon dioxide.

B. lactic acid.

C. oxygen.

D. sodium chloride

73. A Newton is fundamentally a measure of _____ .

A. force.

B. momentum.

C. energy.

D. gravity.

74. Which change does *not* affect enzyme rate?

A. Increase the temperature.

B. Add more substrate.

C. Adjust the pH.

D. Use a larger cell.

75. Which of the following types of rock are made from magma?

A. Fossils

B. Sedimentary

C. Metamorphic

D. Igneous

76. Which of the following is *not* an acceptable way for a student to acknowledge sources in a laboratory report?

A. The student tells his/her teacher what sources s/he used to write the report.

B. The student uses footnotes in the text, with sources cited, but not in correct MLA format.

C. The student uses endnotes in the text, with sources cited, in correct MLA format.

D. The student attaches a separate bibliography, noting each use of sources.

77. Animals with a notochord or backbone are in the phylum

A. arthropoda.

B. chordata.

C. mollusca.

D. mammalia.

78. Which of the following is a correct explanation for scientific 'evolution'?

A. Giraffes need to reach higher for leaves to eat, so their necks stretch. The giraffe babies are then born with longer necks. Eventually, there are more long-necked giraffes in the population.

B. Giraffes with longer necks are able to reach more leaves, so they eat more and have more babies than other giraffes. Eventually, there are more long-necked giraffes in the population.

C. Giraffes want to reach higher for leaves to eat, so they release enzymes into their bloodstream, which in turn causes fetal development of longer-necked giraffes. Eventually, there are more long-necked giraffes in the population.

D. Giraffes with long necks are more attractive to other giraffes, so they get the best mating partners and have more babies. Eventually, there are more long-necked giraffes in the population.

79. Which of the following is a correct definition for 'chemical equilibrium'?

A. Chemical equilibrium is when the forward and backward reaction rates are equal. The reaction may continue to proceed forward and backward.

B. Chemical equilibrium is when the forward and backward reaction rates are equal, and equal to zero. The reaction does not continue.

C. Chemical equilibrium is when there are equal quantities of reactants and products.

D. Chemical equilibrium is when acids and bases neutralize each other fully.

80. Which of the following data sets is properly represented by a bar graph?

A. Number of people choosing to buy cars, vs. Color of car bought.

B. Number of people choosing to buy cars, vs. Age of car customer.

C. Number of people choosing to buy cars, vs. Distance from car lot to customer home.

D. Number of people choosing to buy cars, vs. Time since last car purchase.

81. In a science experiment, a student needs to dispense very small measured amounts of liquid into a well-mixed solution. Which of the following is the best choice for his/her equipment to use?

A. Buret with Buret Stand, Stir-plate, Stirring Rod, Beaker.

B. Buret with Buret Stand, Stir-plate, Beaker.

C. Volumetric Flask, Dropper, Graduated Cylinder, Stirring Rod.

D. Beaker, Graduated Cylinder, Stir-plate.

82. A laboratory balance is most appropriately used to measure the mass of which of the following?

A. Seven paper clips.

B. Three oranges.

C. Two hundred cells.

D. One student's elbow.

83. All of the following are measured in units of length, *except* for:

A. Perimeter.

B. Distance.

C. Radius.

D. Area.

84. What is specific gravity?

A. The mass of an object.

B. The ratio of the density of a substance to the density of water.

C. Density.

D. The pull of the earth's gravity on an object.

85. What is the most accurate description of the Water Cycle?

A. Rain comes from clouds, filling the ocean. The water then evaporates and becomes clouds again.

B. Water circulates from rivers into groundwater and back, while water vapor circulates in the atmosphere.

C. Water is conserved except for chemical or nuclear reactions, and any drop of water could circulate through clouds, rain, ground-water, and surface-water.

D. Weather systems cause chemical reactions to break water into its atoms.

86. The scientific name *Canis familiaris* refers to the animal's _____.

A. kingdom and phylum.

B. genus and species.

C. class and species.

D. type and family.

87. Members of the same animal species _____.

A. look identical.

B. never adapt differently.

C. are able to reproduce with one another.

D. are found in the same location.

88. Which of the following is/are true about scientists?

I. Scientists usually work alone.
II. Scientists usually work with other scientists.
III. Scientists achieve more prestige from new discoveries than from replicating established results.
IV. Scientists keep records of their own work, but do not publish it for outside review.

A. I and IV only.

B. II only.

C. II and III only.

D. I and IV only.

89. What is necessary for ion diffusion to occur spontaneously?

A. Carrier proteins.

B. Energy from an outside source.

C. A concentration gradient.

D. Cell flagellae.

90. All of the following are considered Newton's Laws *except* for:

A. An object in motion will continue in motion unless acted upon by an outside force.

B. For every action force, there is an equal and opposite reaction force.

C. Nature abhors a vacuum.

D. Mass can be considered the ratio of force to acceleration.

91. A cup of hot liquid and a cup of cold liquid are both sitting in a room at comfortable room temperature and humidity. Both cups are thin plastic. Which of the following is a true statement?

A. There will be fog on the outside of the hot liquid cup, and also fog on the outside of the cold liquid cup.

B. There will be fog on the outside of the hot liquid cup, but not on the cold liquid cup.

C. There will be fog on the outside of the cold liquid cup, but not on the hot liquid cup.

D. There will not be fog on the outside of either cup.

92. A ball rolls down a smooth hill. You may ignore air resistance. Which of the following is a true statement?

A. The ball has more energy at the start of its descent than just before it hits the bottom of the hill, because it is higher up at the beginning.

B. The ball has less energy at the start of its descent than just before it hits the bottom of the hill, because it is moving more quickly at the end.

C. The ball has the same energy throughout its descent, because positional energy is converted to energy of motion.

D. The ball has the same energy throughout its descent, because a single object (such as a ball) cannot gain or lose energy.

93. A long silver bar has a temperature of 50 degrees Celsius at one end and 0 degrees Celsius at the other end. The bar will reach thermal equilibrium (barring outside influence) by the process of heat _____.

A. conduction.

B. convection.

C. radiation.

D. phase change.

94. _____ are cracks in the plates of the earth's crust, along which the plates move.

A. Faults.

B. Ridges.

C. Earthquakes.

D. Volcanoes.

95. Fossils are usually found in _____ rock.

A. igneous.

B. sedimentary.

C. metamorphic.

D. cumulus.

96. Which of the following is *not* a common type of acid in 'acid rain' or acidified surface water?

A. Nitric acid.

B. Sulfuric acid.

C. Carbonic acid.

D. Hydrofluoric acid.

97. Which of the following is *not* true about phase change in matter?

A. Solid water and liquid ice can coexist at water's freezing point.

B. At 7 degrees Celsius, water is always in liquid phase.

C. Matter changes phase when enough energy is gained or lost.

D. Different phases of matter are characterized by differences in molecular motion.

98. Which of the following is the longest (largest) unit of geological time?

A. Solar Year.

B. Epoch.

C. Period.

D. Era.

99. Extensive use of antibacterial soap has been found to increase the virulence of certain infections in hospitals. Which of the following might be an explanation for this phenomenon?

A. Antibacterial soaps do not kill viruses.

B. Antibacterial soaps do not incorporate the same antibiotics used as medicine.

C. Antibacterial soaps kill a lot of bacteria, and only the hardiest ones survive to reproduce.

D. Antibacterial soaps can be very drying to the skin.

100. Which of the following is a correct explanation for astronaut 'weightlessness'?

A. Astronauts continue to feel the pull of gravity in space, but they are so far from planets that the force is small.

B. Astronauts continue to feel the pull of gravity in space, but spacecraft have such powerful engines that those forces dominate, reducing effective weight.

C. Astronauts do not feel the pull of gravity in space, because space is a vacuum.

D. Astronauts do not feel the pull of gravity in space, because black hole forces dominate the force field, reducing their masses.

101. The theory of 'sea floor spreading' explains _____.

A. the shapes of the continents.

B. how continents collide.

C. how continents move apart.

D. how continents sink to become part of the ocean floor.

102. Which of the following animals are most likely to live in a tropical rain forest?

A. Reindeer.

B. Monkeys.

C. Puffins.

D. Bears.

103. Which of the following is *not* a type of volcano?

A. Shield Volcanoes.

B. Composite Volcanoes.

C. Stratus Volcanoes.

D. Cinder Cone Volcanoes.

104. Which of the following is *not* a property of metalloids?

A. Metalloids are solids at standard temperature and pressure.

B. Metalloids can conduct electricity to a limited extent.

C. Metalloids are found in groups 13 through 17.

D. Metalloids all favor ionic bonding.

105. Which of these is a true statement about loamy soil?

A. Loamy soil is gritty and porous.

B. Loamy soil is smooth and a good barrier to water.

C. Loamy soil is hostile to microorganisms.

D. Loamy soil is velvety and clumpy.

106. Lithification refers to the process by which unconsolidated sediments aretransformed into _____.

A. metamorphic rocks.

B. sedimentary rocks.

C. igneous rocks.

D. lithium oxide.

107. Igneous rocks can be classified according to which of the following?

A. Texture.

B. Composition.

C. Formation process.

D. All of the above.

108. Which of the following is the most accurate definition of a non-renewable resource?

A. A nonrenewable resource is never replaced once used.

B. A nonrenewable resource is replaced on a timescale that is very long relative to human life-spans.

C. A nonrenewable resource is a resource that can only be manufactured by humans.

D. A nonrenewable resource is a species that has already become extinct.

109. The theory of 'continental drift' is supported by which of the following?

A. The way the shapes of South America and Europe fit together.

B. The way the shapes of Europe and Asia fit together.

C. The way the shapes of South America and Africa fit together.

D. The way the shapes of North America and Antarctica fit together.

110. When water falls to a cave floor and evaporates, it may deposit calcium carbonate. This process leads to the formation of which of the following?

A. Stalactites.

B. Stalagmites.

C. Fault lines.

D. Sedimentary rocks.

111. A child has type O blood. Her father has type A blood, and her mother has type B blood. What are the genotypes of the father and mother, respectively?

A. AO and BO.

B. AA and AB.

C. OO and BO.

D. AO and BB.

112. Which of the following is the best definition for 'meteorite'?

A. A meteorite is a mineral composed of mica and feldspar.

B. A meteorite is material from outer space, that has struck the earth's surface.

C. A meteorite is an element that has properties of both metals and nonmetals.

D. A meteorite is a very small unit of length measurement.

113. A white flower is crossed with a red flower. Which of the following is a sign of incomplete dominance?

A. Pink flowers.

B. Red flowers.

C. White flowers.

D. No flowers.

114. What is the source for most of the United States' drinking water?

A. Desalinated ocean water.

B. Surface water (lakes, streams, mountain runoff).

C. Rainfall into municipal reservoirs.

D. Groundwater.

115. Which is the correct sequence of insect development?

A. Egg, pupa, larva, adult.

B. Egg, larva, pupa, adult.

C. Egg, adult, larva, pupa.

D. Pupa, egg, larva, adult.

116. A wrasse (fish) cleans the teeth of other fish by eating away plaque. This is an example of _____ between the fish.

A. parasitism.

B. symbiosis (mutualism).

C. competition.

D. predation.

117. What is the main obstacle to using nuclear fusion for obtaining electricity?

A. Nuclear fusion produces much more pollution than nuclear fission.

B. There is no obstacle; most power plants us nuclear fusion today.

C. Nuclear fusion requires very high temperature and activation energy.

D. The fuel for nuclear fusion is extremely expensive.

118. Which of the following is a true statement about radiation exposure and air travel?

A. Air travel exposes humans to radiation, but the level is not significant for most people.

B. Air travel exposes humans to so much radiation that it is recommended as a method of cancer treatment.

C. Air travel does not expose humans to radiation.

D. Air travel may or may not expose humans to radiation, but it has not yet been determined.

119. Which process(es) result(s) in a haploid chromosome number?

A. Mitosis.

B. Meiosis.

C. Both mitosis and meiosis.

D. Neither mitosis nor meiosis.

120. Which of the following is *not* a member of Kingdom Fungi?

A. Mold.

B. Blue-green algae.

C. Mildew.

D. Mushrooms.

121. Which of the following organisms use spores to reproduce?

A. Fish.

B. Flowering plants.

C. Conifers.

D. Ferns.

122. What is the main difference between the 'condensation hypothesis' and the 'tidal hypothesis' for the origin of the solar system?

A. The tidal hypothesis can be tested, but the condensation hypothesis cannot.

B. The tidal hypothesis proposes a near collision of two stars pulling on each other, but the condensation hypothesis proposes condensation of rotating clouds of dust and gas.

C. The tidal hypothesis explains how tides began on planets such as Earth, but the condensation hypothesis explains how water vapor became liquid on Earth.

D. The tidal hypothesis is based on Aristotelian physics, but the condensation hypothesis is based on Newtonian mechanics.

123. Which of the following units is *not* a measure of distance?

A. AU (astronomical unit).

B. Light year.

C. Parsec.

D. Lunar year.

124. The salinity of ocean water is closest to _____ .

A. 0.035 %

B. 0.35 %

C. 3.5 %

D. 35 %

125. Which of the following will not change in a chemical reaction?

A. Number of moles of products.

B. Atomic number of one of the reactants.

C. Mass (in grams) of one of the reactants.

D. Rate of reaction.

Answer Key

1. B	26. A	51. D	76. A	101. C
2. A	27. B	52. D	77. B	102. B
3. A	28. D	53. B	78. B	103. C
4. C	29. B	54. B	79. A	104. D
5. B	30. B	55. A	80. A	105. D
6. C	31. C	56. B	81. B	106. B
7. D	32. C	57. B	82. A	107. D
8. C	33. D	58. A	83. D	108. B
9. C	34. A	59. A	84. B	109. C
10. B	35. B	60. C	85. C	110. B
11. A	36. D	61. C	86. B	111. A
12. C	37. A	62. A	87. C	112. B
13. C	38. B	63. B	88. C	113. A
14. B	39. C	64. A	89. C	114. D
15. B	40. A	65. C	90. C	115. B
16. B	41. D	66. D	91. C	116. B
17. A	42. A	67. C	92. C	117. C
18. C	43. B	68. D	93. A	118. A
19. C	44. A	69. B	94. A	119. B
20. D	45. C	70. C	95. B	120. B
21. C	46. C	71. B	96. D	121. D
22. B	47. B	72. B	97. B	122. B
23. A	48. D	73. A	98. D	123. D
24. A	49. B	74. D	99. C	124. C
25. A	50. A	75. D	100. A	125. B

Sample Questions with Rationale

1. After an experiment, the scientist states that s/he believes a change in color is due to a change in pH. This is an example of

A. observing.

B. inferring.

C. measuring.

D. classifying.

B. Inferring.

To answer this question, note that the scientist has observed a change in color, and has then made a guess as to its reason. This is an example of inferring. The scientist has not measured or classified in this case. Although s/he has observed [the color change], the explanation of this observation is **inferring (B)**.

2. When is a hypothesis formed?

A. Before the data is taken.

B. After the data is taken.

C. After the data is analyzed.

D. While the data is being graphed.

A. Before the data is taken.

A hypothesis is an educated guess, made before undertaking an experiment. The hypothesis is then evaluated based on the observed data. Therefore, the hypothesis must be formed before the data is taken, not during or after the experiment. This is consistent only with **answer (A)**.

TEACHER CERTIFICATION STUDY GUIDE

3. Who determines the laws regarding the use of safety glasses in the classroom?

A. The state government.

B. The school site.

C. The federal government.

D. The local district.

A. The state government.

Health and safety regulations are set by the state government, and apply to all school districts. Federal regulations may accompany specific federal grants, and local districts or school sites may enact local guidelines that are stricter than the state standards. All schools, however, must abide by safety precautions as set by state government. This is consistent only with **answer (A)**.

4. If one inch equals 2.54 centimeters, how many millimeters are in 1.5 feet? (Approximately)

A. 18

B. 1800

C. 460

D. 4600

C. 460

To solve this problem, note that if one inch is 2.54 centimeters, then 1.5 feet (which is 18 inches), must be (18)(2.54) centimeters, i.e. approximately 46 centimeters. Because there are ten millimeters in a centimeter, this is approximately 460 millimeters:

(1.5 ft) (12 in/ft) (2.54 cm/in) (10 mm/cm) = (1.5) (12) (2.54) (10) mm = 457.2 mm

This is consistent only with **answer (C)**.

5. Which of the following instruments measures wind speed?

A. Barometer.

B. Anemometer.

C. Thermometer.

D. Weather Vane.

B. Anemometer.

An anemometer is a device to measure wind speed, while a barometer measures pressure, a thermometer measures temperature, and a weather vane indicates wind direction. This is consistent only with **answer (B).**

If you chose "barometer," here is an old physics joke to console you:

A physics teacher asks a student the following question:
"Suppose you want to find out the height of a building, and the only tool you have is a barometer. How could you find out the height?"
(The teacher hopes that the student will remember that pressure is inversely proportional to height, and will measure the pressure at the top of the building and then use the data to calculate the height of the building.)
"Well," says the student, "I could tie a string to the barometer and lower it from the top of the building, and then measure the amount of string required."
"You could," answers the teacher, "but try to think of a method that uses your physics knowledge from our class."
"All right," replies the student, "I could drop the barometer from the roof and measure the time it takes to fall, and then use free-fall equations to calculate the height from which it fell."
"Yes," says the teacher, "but what about using the barometer per se?"
"Oh," answers the student, "I could find the building superintendent, and offer to exchange the barometer for a set of blueprints, and look up the height!"

TEACHER CERTIFICATION STUDY GUIDE

6. Sonar works by _____

A. timing how long it takes sound to reach a certain speed.

B. bouncing sound waves between two metal plates.

C. bouncing sound waves off an object and timing how long it takes for the sound to return.

D. evaluating the motion and amplitude of sound.

C. Bouncing sound waves off an object and timing how long it takes for the sound to return.

Sonar is used to measure distances. Sound waves are sent out, and the time is measured for the sound to hit an obstacle and bounce back. By using the known speed of sound, observers (or machines) can calculate the distance to the obstacle. This is consistent only with **answer (C)**.

7. The measure of the pull of Earth's gravity on an object is called

A. mass number.

B. atomic number.

C. mass.

D. weight.

D. Weight.

To answer this question, recall that mass number is the total number of protons and neutrons in an atom, atomic number is the number of protons in an atom, and mass is the amount of matter in an object. The only remaining **choice is (D)**, weight, which is correct because weight is the force of gravity on an object.

TEACHER CERTIFICATION STUDY GUIDE

8. Which reaction below is a decomposition reaction?

A. $HCl + NaOH \rightarrow NaCl + H_2O$

B. $C + O_2 \rightarrow CO_2$

C. $2H_2O \rightarrow 2H_2 + O_2$

D. $CuSO_4 + Fe \rightarrow FeSO_4 + Cu$

C. $2H_2O \rightarrow 2H_2 + O_2$

To answer this question, recall that a decomposition reaction is one in which there are fewer reactants (on the left) than products (on the right). This is consistent only with **answer (C)**. Meanwhile, note that answer (A) shows a double-replacement reaction (in which two sets of ions switch bonds), answer (B) shows a synthesis reaction (in which there are fewer products than reactants), and answer (D) shows a single-replacement reaction (in which one substance replaces another in its bond, but the other does not get a new bond).

9. The Law of Conservation of Energy states that

A. there must be the same number of products and reactants in any chemical equation.

B. objects always fall toward large masses such as planets.

C. energy is neither created nor destroyed, but may change form.

D. lights must be turned off when not in use, by state regulation.

C. Energy is neither created nor destroyed, but may change form.

Answer (C) is a summary of the Law of Conservation of Energy (for non-nuclear reactions). In other words, energy can be transformed into various forms such as kinetic, potential, electric, or heat energy, but the total amount of energy remains constant. Answer (A) is untrue, as demonstrated by many synthesis and decomposition reactions. Answers (B) and (D) may be sensible, but they are not relevant in this case. Therefore, the **answer is (C).**

10. Which parts of an atom are located inside the nucleus?

A. Protons and Electrons.

B. Protons and Neutrons.

C. Protons only.

D. Neutrons only.

B. Protons and Neutrons.

Protons and neutrons are located in the nucleus, while electrons move around outside the nucleus. This is consistent only with **answer (B)**.

11. The elements in the modern Periodic Table are arranged

A. in numerical order by atomic number.

B. randomly.

C. in alphabetical order by chemical symbol.

D. in numerical order by atomic mass.

A. In numerical order by atomic number.

Although the first periodic tables were arranged by atomic mass, the modern table is arranged by atomic number, i.e. the number of protons in each element. (This allows the element list to be complete and unique.) The elements are not arranged either randomly or in alphabetical order. The answer to this question is **therefore (A)**.

TEACHER CERTIFICATION STUDY GUIDE

12. Carbon bonds with hydrogen by

A. ionic bonding.

B. non-polar covalent bonding.

C. polar covalent bonding.

D. strong nuclear force.

C. Polar covalent bonding.

Each carbon atom contains four valence electrons, while each hydrogen atom contains one valence electron. A carbon atom can bond with one or more hydrogen atoms, such that two electrons are shared in each bond. This is covalent bonding, because the electrons are shared. (In ionic bonding, atoms must gain or lose electrons to form ions. The ions are then electrically attracted in oppositely-charged pairs.) Covalent bonds are always polar when between two non-identical atoms, so this bond must be polar. ("Polar" means that the electrons are shared unequally, forming a pair of partial charges, i.e. poles.) In any case, the strong nuclear force is not relevant to this problem. The answer to this question is **therefore (C).**

13. Vinegar is an example of a _____

A. strong acid.

B. strong base.

C. weak acid.

D. weak base.

C. Weak acid.

The main ingredient in vinegar is acetic acid, a weak acid. Vinegar is a useful acid in science classes, because it makes a frothy reaction with bases such as baking soda (e.g. in the quintessential volcano model). Vinegar is not a strong acid, such as hydrochloric acid, because it does not dissociate as fully or cause as much corrosion. It is not a base. Therefore, the **answer is (C)**.

TEACHER CERTIFICATION STUDY GUIDE

14. Which of the following is not a nucleotide?

A. Adenine.

B. Alanine.

C. Cytosine.

D. Guanine.

B. Alanine.

Alanine is an amino acid. Adenine, cytosine, guanine, thymine, and uracil are nucleotides. The correct **answer is (B)**.

15. When measuring the volume of water in a graduated cylinder, where does one read the measurement?

A. At the highest point of the liquid.

B. At the bottom of the meniscus curve.

C. At the closest mark to the top of the liquid.

D. At the top of the plastic safety ring.

B. At the bottom of the meniscus curve.

To measure water in glass, you must look at the top surface at eye-level, and ascertain the location of the bottom of the meniscus (the curved surface at the top of the water). The meniscus forms because water molecules adhere to the sides of the glass, which is a slightly stronger force than their cohesion to each other. This leads to a U-shaped top of the liquid column, the bottom of which gives the most accurate volume measurement. (Other liquids have different forces, e.g. mercury in glass, which has a convex meniscus.) This is consistent only with **answer (B)**.

16. A duck's webbed feet are examples of

A. mimicry.

B. structural adaptation.

C. protective resemblance.

D. protective coloration.

B. Structural adaptation.

Ducks (and other aquatic birds) have webbed feet, which makes them more efficient swimmers. This is most likely due to evolutionary patterns where webbed-footed-birds were more successful at feeding and reproducing, and eventually became the majority of aquatic birds. Because the structure of the duck adapted to its environment over generations, this is termed 'structural adaptation'. Mimicry, protective resemblance, and protective coloration refer to other evolutionary mechanisms for survival. The answer to this question is therefore **(B)**.

17. What cell organelle contains the cell's stored food?

A. Vacuoles.

B. Golgi Apparatus.

C. Ribosomes.

D. Lysosomes.

A. Vacuoles.

In a cell, the sub-parts are called organelles. Of these, the vacuoles hold stored food (and water and pigments). The Golgi Apparatus sorts molecules from other parts of the cell; the ribosomes are sites of protein synthesis; the lysosomes contain digestive enzymes. This is consistent only with **answer (A)**.

18. The first stage of mitosis is called _____

A. telophase.

B. anaphase.

C. prophase.

D. mitophase.

C. Prophase.

In mitosis, the division of somatic cells, prophase is the stage where the cell enters mitosis. The four stages of mitosis, in order, are: prophase, metaphase, anaphase, and telophase. ("Mitophase" is not one of the steps.) During prophase, the cell begins the nonstop process of division. Its chromatin condenses, its nucleolus disappears, the nuclear membrane breaks apart, mitotic spindles form, its cytoskeleton breaks down, and centrioles push the spindles apart. Note that interphase, the stage where chromatin is loose, chromosomes are replicated, and cell metabolism is occurring, is technically not a stage of mitosis; it is a precursor to cell division.

19. The Doppler Effect is associated most closely with which property of waves?

A. Amplitude.

B. Wavelength.

C. Frequency.

D. Intensity.

C. Frequency.

The Doppler Effect accounts for an apparent increase in frequency when a wave source moves toward a wave receiver or apparent decrease in frequency when a wave source moves away from a wave receiver. (Note that the receiver could also be moving toward or away from the source.) As the wave fronts are released, motion toward the receiver mimics more frequent wave fronts, while motion away from the receiver mimics less frequent wave fronts. Meanwhile, the amplitude, wavelength, and intensity of the wave are not as relevant to this process (although moving closer to a wave source makes it seem more intense). The **answer to this question is therefore (C)**.

20. Viruses are responsible for many human diseases including all of the following *except*

A. influenza.

B. A.I.D.S.

C. the common cold.

D. strep throat.

D. Strep throat.

Influenza, A.I.D.S., and the "common cold" (rhinovirus infection), are all caused by viruses. (This is the reason that doctors should not be pressured to prescribe antibiotics for colds or 'flu—i.e. they will not be effective since the infections are not bacterial.) Strep throat (properly called 'streptococcal throat' and caused by streptococcus bacteria) is not a virus, but a bacterial infection. Thus, the **answer is (D)**.

21. A series of experiments on pea plants formed by _____ showed that two invisible markers existed for each trait, and one marker dominated the other.

A. Pasteur.

B. Watson and Crick.

C. Mendel.

D. Mendeleev.

C. Mendel.

Gregor Mendel was a ninteenth-century Austrian botanist, who derived "laws" governing inherited traits. His work led to the understanding of dominant and recessive traits, carried by biological markers. Mendel cross-bred different kinds of pea plants with varying features and observed the resulting new plants. He showed that genetic characteristics are not passed identically from one generation to the next. (Pasteur, Watson, Crick, and Mendeleev were other scientists with different specialties.) This is consistent only with **answer (C)**.

TEACHER CERTIFICATION STUDY GUIDE

22. Formaldehyde should not be used in school laboratories for the following reason:

A. it smells unpleasant.

B. it is a known carcinogen.

C. it is expensive to obtain.

D. it is an explosive.

B. It is a known carcinogen.

Formaldehyde is a known carcinogen, so it is too dangerous for use in schools. In general, teachers should not use carcinogens in school laboratories. Although formaldehyde also smells unpleasant, a smell alone is not a definitive marker of danger. For example, many people find the smell of vinegar to be unpleasant, but vinegar is considered a very safe classroom/laboratory chemical. Furthermore, some odorless materials are toxic. Formaldehyde is neither particularly expensive nor explosive. Thus, the **answer is (B)**.

23. Amino acids are carried to the ribosome in protein synthesis by:

A. transfer RNA (tRNA).

B. messenger RNA (mRNA).

C. ribosomal RNA (rRNA).

D. transformation RNA (trRNA).

A. Transfer RNA (tRNA).

The job of tRNA is to carry and position amino acids to/on the ribosomes. mRNA copies DNA code and brings it to the ribosomes; rRNA is in the ribosome itself. There is no such thing as trRNA. Thus, the **answer is (A)**.

MID. LEVEL SCIENCE

TEACHER CERTIFICATION STUDY GUIDE

24. When designing a scientific experiment, a student considers all the factors that may influence the results. The process goal is to _____

A. recognize and manipulate independent variables.

B. recognize and record independent variables.

C. recognize and manipulate dependent variables.

D. recognize and record dependent variables.

A. Recognize and manipulate independent variables.

When a student designs a scientific experiment, s/he must decide what to measure, and what independent variables will play a role in the experiment. S/he must determine how to manipulate these independent variables to refine his/her procedure and to prepare for meaningful observations. Although s/he will eventually record dependent variables (D), this does not take place during the experimental design phase. Although the student will likely recognize and record the independent variables (B), this is not the process goal, but a helpful step in manipulating the variables. It is unlikely that the student will manipulate dependent variables directly in his/her experiment (C), or the data would be suspect. Thus, the **answer is (A)**.

25. Since ancient times, people have been entranced with bird flight. What is the key to bird flight?

A. Bird wings are a particular shape and composition.

B. Birds flap their wings quickly enough to propel themselves.

C. Birds take advantage of tailwinds.

D. Birds take advantage of crosswinds.

A. Bird wings are a particular shape and composition.

Bird wings are shaped for wide area, and their bones are very light. This creates a large surface-area-to-mass ratio, enabling birds to glide in air. Birds do flap their wings and float on winds, but none of these is the main reason for their flight ability. Thus, the **answer is (A)**.

TEACHER CERTIFICATION STUDY GUIDE

26. Laboratory researchers have classified fungi as distinct from plants because the cell walls of fungi

A. contain chitin.

B. contain yeast.

C. are more solid.

D. are less solid.

A. Contain chitin.

Kingdom Fungi consists of organisms that are eukaryotic, multicellular, absorptive consumers. They have a chitin cell wall, which is the only universally present feature in fungi that is never present in plants. Thus, the **answer is (A)**.

27. In a fission reactor, "heavy water" is used to _____

A. terminate fission reactions.

B. slow down neutrons and moderate reactions.

C. rehydrate the chemicals.

D. initiate a chain reaction.

B. Slow down neutrons and moderate reactions.

"Heavy water" is used in a nuclear [fission] reactor to slow down neutrons, controlling and moderating the nuclear reactions. It does not terminate the reaction, and it does not initiate the reaction. Also, although the reactor takes advantage of water's other properties (e.g. high specific heat for cooling), the water does not "rehydrate" the chemicals. Therefore, the **answer is (B)**.

28. The transfer of heat by electromagnetic waves is called _____

A. conduction.

B. convection.

C. phase change.

D. radiation.

D. Radiation.

Heat transfer via electromagnetic waves (which can occur even in a vacuum) is called radiation. (Heat can also be transferred by direct contact (conduction), by fluid current (convection), and by matter changing phase, but these are not relevant here.) The answer to this question is **therefore (D)**.

29. When heat is added to most solids, they expand. Why is this the case?

A. The molecules get bigger.

B. The faster molecular motion leads to greater distance between the molecules.

C. The molecules develop greater repelling electric forces.

D. The molecules form a more rigid structure.

B. The faster molecular motion leads to greater distance between the molecules.

The atomic theory of matter states that matter is made up of tiny, rapidly moving particles. These particles move more quickly when warmer, because temperature is a measure of average kinetic energy of the particles. Warmer molecules therefore move further away from each other, with enough energy to separate from each other more often and for greater distances. The individual molecules do not get bigger, by conservation of mass, eliminating answer (A). The molecules do not develop greater repelling electric forces, eliminating answer (C). Occasionally, molecules form a more rigid structure when becoming colder and freezing (such as water)—but this gives rise to the exceptions to heat expansion, so it is not relevant here, eliminating answer (D). Therefore, the **answer is (B)**.

30. The force of gravity on earth causes all bodies in free fall to _____

A. fall at the same speed.

B. accelerate at the same rate.

C. reach the same terminal velocity.

D. move in the same direction.

B. Accelerate at the same rate.

Gravity causes approximately the same acceleration on all falling bodies close to earth's surface. (It is only "approximately" because there are very small variations in the strength of earth's gravitational field.) More massive bodies continue to accelerate at this rate for longer, before their air resistance is great enough to cause terminal velocity, so answers (A) and (C) are eliminated. Bodies on different parts of the planet move in different directions (always toward the center of mass of earth), so answer (D) is eliminated. Thus, the **answer is (B)**.

31. Sound waves are produced by _____

A. pitch.

B. noise.

C. vibrations.

D. sonar.

C. Vibrations.

Sound waves are produced by a vibrating body. The vibrating object moves forward and compresses the air in front of it, then reverses direction so that the pressure on the air is lessened and expansion of the air molecules occurs. The vibrating air molecules move back and forth parallel to the direction of motion of the wave as they pass the energy from adjacent air molecules closer to the source to air molecules farther away from the source. Therefore, the **answer is (C)**.

32. Resistance is measured in units called

A. watts.

B. volts.

C. ohms.

D. current.

C. Ohms.

A watt is a unit of energy. Potential difference is measured in a unit called the volt. Current is the number of electrons per second that flow past a point in a circuit. An ohm is the unit for resistance. The correct **answer is (C)**.

33. Sound can be transmitted in all of the following *except*

A. air.

B. water.

C. diamond.

D. a vacuum.

D. A vacuum.

Sound, a longitudinal wave, is transmitted by vibrations of molecules. Therefore, it can be transmitted through any gas, liquid, or solid. However, it cannot be transmitted through a vacuum, because there are no particles present to vibrate and bump into their adjacent particles to transmit the waves. This is consistent only with **answer (D)**. (It is interesting also to note that sound is actually faster in solids and liquids than in air.)

34. As a train approaches, the whistle sounds

A. higher, because it has a higher apparent frequency.

B. lower, because it has a lower apparent frequency.

C. higher, because it has a lower apparent frequency.

D. lower, because it has a higher apparent frequency.

A. Higher, because it has a higher apparent frequency.

By the Doppler effect, when a source of sound is moving toward an observer, the wave fronts are released closer together, i.e. with a greater apparent frequency. Higher frequency sounds are higher in pitch. This is consistent only with **answer (A)**.

35. The speed of light is different in different materials. This is responsible for _____

A. interference.

B. refraction.

C. reflection.

D. relativity.

B. Refraction.

Refraction (B) is the bending of light because it hits a material at an angle wherein it has a different speed. (This is analogous to a cart rolling on a smooth road. If it hits a rough patch at an angle, the wheel on the rough patch slows down first, leading to a change in direction.) Interference (A) is when light waves interfere with each other to form brighter or dimmer patterns; reflection (C) is when light bounces off a surface; relativity (D) is a general topic related to light speed and its implications, but not specifically indicated here. Therefore, the **answer is (B)**.

TEACHER CERTIFICATION STUDY GUIDE

36. A converging lens produces a real image _____

A. always.

B. never.

C. when the object is within one focal length of the lens.

D. when the object is further than one focal length from the lens.

D. When the object is further than one focal length from the lens.

A converging lens produces a real image whenever the object is far enough from the lens (outside one focal length) so that the rays of light from the object can hit the lens and be focused into a real image on the other side of the lens. When the object is closer than one focal length from the lens, rays of light do not converge on the other side; they diverge. This means that only a virtual image can be formed, i.e. the theoretical place where those diverging rays would have converged if they had originated behind the object. Thus, the correct **answer is (D)**.

37. The electromagnetic radiation with the longest wave length is _____

A. radio waves.

B. red light.

C. X-rays.

D. ultraviolet light.

A. Radio waves.

As one can see on a diagram of the electromagnetic spectrum, radio waves have longer wave lengths (and smaller frequencies) than visible light, which in turn has longer wave lengths than ultraviolet or X-ray radiation. If you did not remember this sequence, you might recall that wave length is inversely proportional to frequency, and that radio waves are considered much less harmful (less energetic, i.e. lower frequency) than ultraviolet or X-ray radiation. The correct answer is **therefore (A)**.

38. Under a 440 power microscope, an object with diameter 0.1 millimeter appears to have diameter _____

A. 4.4 millimeters.

B. 44 millimeters.

C. 440 millimeters.

D. 4400 millimeters.

B. 44 millimeters.

To answer this question, recall that to calculate a new length, you multiply the original length by the magnification power of the instrument. Therefore, the 0.1 millimeter diameter is multiplied by 440. This equals 44, so the image appears to be 44 millimeters in diameter. You could also reason that since a 440 power microscope is considered a "high power" microscope, you would expect a 0.1 millimeter object to appear a few centimeters long. Therefore, the correct **answer is (B)**.

39. To separate blood into blood cells and plasma involves the process of

A. electrophoresis.

B. spectrophotometry.

C. centrifugation.

D. chromatography.

C. Centrifugation.

Electrophoresis uses electrical charges of molecules to separate them according to their size. Spectrophotometry uses percent light absorbance to measure a color change, thus giving qualitative data a quantitative value. Chromatography uses the principles of capillarity to separate substances. Centrifugation involves spinning substances at a high speed. The more dense part of a solution will settle to the bottom of the test tube, where the lighter material will stay on top. The **answer is (C).**

TEACHER CERTIFICATION STUDY GUIDE

40. Experiments may be done with any of the following animals except

A. birds.

B. invertebrates.

C. lower order life.

D. frogs.

A. Birds.

No dissections may be performed on living mammalian vertebrates or birds. Lower order life and invertebrates may be used. Biological experiments may be done with all animals except mammalian vertebrates or birds. Therefore the **answer is (A)**.

41. For her first project of the year, a student is designing a science experiment to test the effects of light and water on plant growth. You should recommend that she _____

A. manipulate the temperature also.

B. manipulate the water pH also.

C. determine the relationship between light and water unrelated to plant growth.

D. omit either water or light as a variable.

D. Omit either water or light as a variable.

As a science teacher for middle-school-aged kids, it is important to reinforce the idea of 'constant' vs. 'variable' in science experiments. At this level, it is wisest to have only one variable examined in each science experiment. (Later, students can hold different variables constant while investigating others.) Therefore it is counterproductive to add in other variables (answers (A) or (B)). It is also irrelevant to determine the light-water interactions aside from plant growth (C). So the only possible **answer is (D)**.

MID. LEVEL SCIENCE

42. In a laboratory report, what is the abstract?

A. The abstract is a summary of the report, and is the first section of the report.

B. The abstract is a summary of the report, and is the last section of the report.

C. The abstract is predictions for future experiments, and is the first section of the report.

D. The abstract is predictions for future experiments, and is the last section of the report.

A. The abstract is a summary of the report, and is the first section of the report.

In a laboratory report, the abstract is the section that summarizes the entire report (often containing one representative sentence from each section). It appears at the very beginning of the report, even before the introduction, often on its own page (instead of a title page). This format is consistent with articles in scientific journals. Therefore, the **answer is (A)**.

43. What is the scientific method?

A. It is the process of doing an experiment and writing a laboratory report.

B. It is the process of using open inquiry and repeatable results to establish theories.

C. It is the process of reinforcing scientific principles by confirming results.

D. It is the process of recording data and observations.

B. It is the process of using open inquiry and repeatable results to establish theories.

Scientific research often includes elements from answers (A), (C), and (D), but the basic underlying principle of the scientific method is that people ask questions and do repeatable experiments to answer those questions and develop informed theories of why and how things happen. Therefore, the best **answer is (B)**.

44. Identify the control in the following experiment: A student had four corn plants and was measuring photosynthetic rate (by measuring growth mass). Half of the plants were exposed to full (constant) sunlight, and the other half were kept in 50% (constant) sunlight.

A. The control is a set of plants grown in full (constant) sunlight.

B. The control is a set of plants grown in 50% (constant) sunlight.

C. The control is a set of plants grown in the dark.

D. The control is a set of plants grown in a mixture of natural levels of sunlight.

A. The control is a set of plants grown in full (constant) sunlight.

In this experiment, the goal was to measure how two different amounts of sunlight affected plant growth. The control in any experiment is the 'base case,' or the usual situation without a change in variable. Because the control must be studied alongside the variable, answers (C) and (D) are omitted (because they were not in the experiment). The **better answer of (A) and (B) is (A)**, because usually plants are assumed to have the best growth and their usual growing circumstances in full sunlight. This is particularly true for crops like the corn plants in this question.

45. In an experiment measuring the growth of bacteria at different temperatures, what is the independent variable?

A. Number of bacteria.

B. Growth rate of bacteria.

C. Temperature.

D. Light intensity.

C. Temperature.

To answer this question, recall that the independent variable in an experiment is the entity that is changed by the scientist, in order to observe the effects (the dependent variable(s)). In this experiment, temperature is changed in order to measure growth of bacteria, so **(C) is the answer**. Note that answer (A) is the dependent variable, and neither (B) nor (D) is directly relevant to the question.

46. A scientific law _____

A. proves scientific accuracy.

B. may never be broken.

C. may be revised in light of new data.

D. is the result of one excellent experiment.

C. May be revised in light of new data.

A scientific law is the same as a scientific theory, except that it has lasted for longer, and has been supported by more extensive data. Therefore, such a law may be revised in light of new data, and may be broken by that new data. Furthermore, a scientific law is always the result of many experiments, and never 'proves' anything but rather is implied or supported by various results. Therefore, the **answer must be (C)**.

47. Which is the correct order of methodology?

1. collecting data
2. planning a controlled experiment
3. drawing a conclusion
4. hypothesizing a result
5. re-visiting a hypothesis to answer a question

A. 1,2,3,4,5

B. 4,2,1,3,5

C. 4,5,1,3,2

D. 1,3,4,5,2

B. 4,2,1,3,5

The correct methodology for the scientific method is first to make a meaningful hypothesis (educated guess), then plan and execute a controlled experiment to test that hypothesis. Using the data collected in that experiment, the scientist then draws conclusions and attempts to answer the original question related to the hypothesis. This is consistent only with **answer (B)**.

48. Which is the most desirable tool to use to heat substances in a middle school laboratory?

A. Alcohol burner.

B. Freestanding gas burner.

C. Bunsen burner.

D. Hot plate.

D. Hot plate.

Due to safety considerations, the use of open flame should be minimized, so a hot plate is the best choice. Any kind of burner may be used with proper precautions, but it is difficult to maintain a completely safe middle school environment. Therefore, the best **answer is (D)**.

49. Newton's Laws are taught in science classes because _____.

A. they are the correct analysis of inertia, gravity, and forces.

B. they are a close approximation to correct physics, for usual Earth conditions.

C. they accurately incorporate Relativity into studies of forces.

D. Newton was a well-respected scientist in his time.

B. They are a close approximation to correct physics, for usual Earth conditions.

Although Newton's Laws are often taught as fully correct for inertia, gravity, and forces, it is important to realize that Einstein's work (and that of others) has indicated that Newton's Laws are reliable only at speeds much lower than that of light. This is reasonable, though, for most middle- and high-school applications. At speeds close to the speed of light, Relativity considerations must be used. Therefore, the only correct **answer is (B)**.

50. Which of the following is most accurate?

A. Mass is always constant; Weight may vary by location.

B. Mass and Weight are both always constant.

C. Weight is always constant; Mass may vary by location.

D. Mass and Weight may both vary by location.

A. Mass is always constant; Weight may vary by location.

When considering situations exclusive of nuclear reactions, mass is constant (mass, the amount of matter in a system, is conserved). Weight, on the other hand, is the force of gravity on an object, which is subject to change due to changes in the gravitational field and/or the location of the object. Thus, the **best answer is (A)**.

51. Chemicals should be stored _____

A. in the principal's office.

B. in a dark room.

C. in an off-site research facility.

D. according to their reactivity with other substances.

D. According to their reactivity with other substances.

Chemicals should be stored with other chemicals of similar properties (e.g. acids with other acids), to reduce the potential for either hazardous reactions in the store-room, or mistakes in reagent use. Certainly, chemicals should not be stored in anyone's office, and the light intensity of the room is not very important because light-sensitive chemicals are usually stored in dark containers. In fact, good lighting is desirable in a store-room, so that labels can be read easily. Chemicals may be stored off-site, but that makes their use inconvenient. Therefore, the best **answer is (D)**.

52. Which of the following is the worst choice for a school laboratory activity?

A. A genetics experiment tracking the fur color of mice.

B. Dissection of a preserved fetal pig.

C. Measurement of goldfish respiration rate at different temperatures.

D. Pithing a frog to watch the circulatory system.

D. Pithing a frog to watch the circulatory system.

While any use of animals (alive or dead) must be done with care to respect ethics and laws, it is possible to perform choices (A), (B), or (C) with due care. (Note that students will need significant assistance and maturity to perform these experiments.) However, modern practice precludes pithing animals (causing partial brain death while allowing some systems to function), as inhumane. Therefore, the answer to this **question is (D)**.

53. Who should be notified in the case of a serious chemical spill?

A. The custodian.

B. The fire department or other municipal authority.

C. The science department chair.

D. The School Board.

B. The fire department or other municipal authority.

Although the custodian may help to clean up laboratory messes, and the science department chair should be involved in discussions of ways to avoid spills, a serious chemical spill may require action by the fire department or other trained emergency personnel. It is best to be safe by notifying them in case of a serious chemical accident. Therefore, the **best answer is (B)**.

54. A scientist exposes mice to cigarette smoke, and notes that their lungs develop tumors. Mice that were not exposed to the smoke do not develop as many tumors. Which of the following conclusions may be drawn from these results?

I. Cigarette smoke causes lung tumors.
II. Cigarette smoke exposure has a positive correlation with lung tumors in mice.
III. Some mice are predisposed to develop lung tumors.
IV. Mice are often a good model for humans in scientific research.

A. I and II only.

B. II only.

C. I, II, and III only.

D. II and IV only.

B. II only.

Although cigarette smoke has been found to cause lung tumors (and many other problems), this particular experiment shows only that there is a positive correlation between smoke exposure and tumor development in these mice. It may be true that some mice are more likely to develop tumors than others, which is why a control group of identical mice should have been used for comparison. Mice are often used to model human reactions, but this is as much due to their low financial and emotional cost as it is due to their being a "good model" for humans. Therefore, the **answer must be (B)**.

55. In which situation would a science teacher be legally liable?

A. The teacher leaves the classroom for a telephone call and a student slips and injures him/herself.

B. A student removes his/her goggles and gets acid in his/her eye.

C. A faulty gas line in the classroom causes a fire.

D. A student cuts him/herself with a dissection scalpel.

A. The teacher leaves the classroom for a telephone call and a student slips and injures him/herself.

Teachers are required to exercise a "reasonable duty of care" for their students. Accidents may happen (e.g. (D)), or students may make poor decisions (e.g. (B)), or facilities may break down (e.g. (C)). However, the teacher has the responsibility to be present and to do his/her best to create a safe and effective learning environment. Therefore, the **answer is (A)**.

56. Which of these is the best example of 'negligence'?

A. A teacher fails to give oral instructions to those with reading disabilities.

B. A teacher fails to exercise ordinary care to ensure safety in the classroom.

C. A teacher displays inability to supervise a large group of students.

D. A teacher reasonably anticipates that an event may occur, and plans accordingly.

B. A teacher fails to exercise ordinary care to ensure safety in the classroom.

'Negligence' is the failure to "exercise ordinary care" to ensure an appropriate and safe classroom environment. It is best for a teacher to meet all special requirements for disabled students, and to be good at supervising large groups. However, if a teacher can prove that s/he has done a reasonable job to ensure a safe and effective learning environment, then it is unlikely that she/he would be found negligent. Therefore, **the answer is (B)**.

TEACHER CERTIFICATION STUDY GUIDE

57. Which item should always be used when handling glassware?

A. Tongs.

B. Safety goggles.

C. Gloves.

D. Buret stand.

B. Safety goggles.

Safety goggles are the single most important piece of safety equipment in the laboratory, and should be used any time a scientist is using glassware, heat, or chemicals. Other equipment (e.g. tongs, gloves, or even a buret stand) has its place for various applications. However, the most important is safety goggles. Therefore, the **answer is (B)**.

58. Which of the following is *not* a necessary characteristic of living things?

A. Movement.

B. Reduction of local entropy.

C. Ability to cause local energy form changes.

D. Reproduction.

A. Movement.

There are many definitions of "life," but in all cases, a living organism reduces local entropy, changes chemical energy into other forms, and reproduces. Not all living things move, however, so the correct **answer is (A)**.

59. What are the most significant and prevalent elements in the biosphere?

A. Carbon, Hydrogen, Oxygen, Nitrogen, Phosphorus.

B. Carbon, Hydrogen, Sodium, Iron, Calcium.

C. Carbon, Oxygen, Sulfur, Manganese, Iron.

D. Carbon, Hydrogen, Oxygen, Nickel, Sodium, Nitrogen.

A. Carbon, Hydrogen, Oxygen, Nitrogen, Phosphorus.

Organic matter (and life as we know it) is based on Carbon atoms, bonded to Hydrogen and Oxygen. Nitrogen and Phosphorus are the next most significant elements, followed by Sulfur and then trace nutrients such as Iron, Sodium, Calcium, and others. Therefore, the **answer is (A)**. If you know that the formula for any carbohydrate contains Carbon, Hydrogen, and Oxygen, that will help you narrow the choices to (A) and (D) in any case.

60. All of the following measure energy *except* for _____

A. joules.

B. calories.

C. watts.

D. ergs.

C. Watts.

Energy units must be dimensionally equivalent to (force)x(length), which equals (mass)x(length squared)/(time squared). Joules, Calories, and Ergs are all metric measures of energy. Joules are the SI units of energy, while Calories are used to allow water to have a Specific Heat of one unit. Ergs are used in the 'cgs' (centimeter-gram-second) system, for smaller quantities. Watts, however, are units of power, i.e. Joules per Second. Therefore, the **answer is (C)**.

TEACHER CERTIFICATION STUDY GUIDE

61. Identify the correct sequence of organization of living things from lower to higher order:

A. Cell, Organelle, Organ, Tissue, System, Organism.

B. Cell, Tissue, Organ, Organelle, System, Organism.

C. Organelle, Cell, Tissue, Organ, System, Organism.

D. Organelle, Tissue, Cell, Organ, System, Organism.

C. Organelle, Cell, Tissue, Organ, System, Organism.

Organelles are parts of the cell; cells make up tissue, which makes up organs. Organs work together in systems (e.g. the respiratory system), and the organism is the living thing as a whole. Therefore, the **answer must be (C)**.

62. Which kingdom is comprised of organisms made of one cell with no nuclear membrane?

A. Monera.

B. Protista.

C. Fungi.

D. Algae.

A. Monera.

To answer this question, first note that algae are not a kingdom of their own. Some algae are in monera, the kingdom that consists of unicellular prokaryotes with no true nucleus. Protista and fungi are both eukaryotic, with true nuclei, and are sometimes multi-cellular. Therefore, the **answer is (A)**.

63. Which of the following is found in the least abundance in organic molecules?

A. Phosphorus.

B. Potassium.

C. Carbon.

D. Oxygen.

B. Potassium.

Organic molecules consist mainly of Carbon, Hydrogen, and Oxygen, with significant amounts of Nitrogen, Phosphorus, and often Sulfur. Other elements, such as Potassium, are present in much smaller quantities. Therefore, the **answer is (B)**. If you were not aware of this ranking, you might have been able to eliminate Carbon and Oxygen because of their prevalence, in any case.

64. Catalysts assist reactions by _____

A. lowering effective activation energy.

B. maintaining precise pH levels.

C. keeping systems at equilibrium.

D. adjusting reaction speed.

A. Lowering effective activation energy.

Chemical reactions can be enhanced or accelerated by catalysts, which are present both with reactants and with products. They induce the formation of activated complexes, thereby lowering the effective activation energy—so that less energy is necessary for the reaction to begin. Although this often makes reactions faster, answer (D) is not as good a choice as the more generally applicable **answer (A)**, which is correct.

65. Accepted procedures for preparing solutions should be made with

A. alcohol.

B. hydrochloric acid.

C. distilled water.

D. tap water.

C. Distilled water.

Alcohol and hydrochloric acid should never be used to make solutions unless instructed to do so. All solutions should be made with distilled water as tap water contains dissolved particles which may affect the results of an experiment. The correct **answer is (C).**

66. Enzymes speed up reactions by _____

A. utilizing ATP.

B. lowering pH, allowing reaction speed to increase.

C. increasing volume of substrate.

D. lowering energy of activation.

D. Lowering energy of activation.

Because enzymes are catalysts, they work the same way—they cause the formation of activated chemical complexes, which require a lower activation energy. Therefore, the **answer is (D).** ATP is an energy source for cells, and pH or volume changes may or may not affect reaction rate, so these answers can be eliminated.

67. When you step out of the shower, the floor feels colder on your feet than the bathmat. Which of the following is the correct explanation for this phenomenon?

A. The floor is colder than the bathmat.

B. Your feet have a chemical reaction with the floor, but not the bathmat.

C. Heat is conducted more easily into the floor.

D. Water is absorbed from your feet into the bathmat.

C. Heat is conducted more easily into the floor.

When you step out of the shower and onto a surface, the surface is most likely at room temperature, regardless of its composition (eliminating answer (A)). Your feet feel cold when heat is transferred from them to the surface, which happens more easily on a hard floor than a soft bathmat. This is because of differences in specific heat (the energy required to change temperature, which varies by material). Therefore, the **answer must be (C)**, i.e. heat is conducted more easily into the floor from your feet.

68. Which of the following is *not* considered ethical behavior for a scientist?

A. Using unpublished data and citing the source.

B. Publishing data before other scientists have had a chance to replicate results.

C. Collaborating with other scientists from different laboratories.

D. Publishing work with an incomplete list of citations.

D. Publishing work with an incomplete list of citations.

One of the most important ethical principles for scientists is to cite all sources of data and analysis when publishing work. It is reasonable to use unpublished data (A), as long as the source is cited. Most science is published before other scientists replicate it (B), and frequently scientists collaborate with each other, in the same or different laboratories (C). These are all ethical choices. However, publishing work without the appropriate citations, is unethical. Therefore, the **answer is (D).**

69. The chemical equation for water formation is: $2H_2 + O_2 \rightarrow 2H_2O$. Which of the following is an *incorrect* interpretation of this equation?

A. Two moles of hydrogen gas and one mole of oxygen gas combine to make two moles of water.

B. Two grams of hydrogen gas and one gram of oxygen gas combine to make two grams of water.

C. Two molecules of hydrogen gas and one molecule of oxygen gas combine to make two molecules of water.

D. Four atoms of hydrogen (combined as a diatomic gas) and two atoms of oxygen (combined as a diatomic gas) combine to make two molecules of water.

B. Two grams of hydrogen gas and one gram of oxygen gas combine to make two grams of water.

In any chemical equation, the coefficients indicate the relative proportions of molecules (or atoms), or of moles of molecules. They do not refer to mass, because chemicals combine in repeatable combinations of molar ratio (i.e. number of moles), but vary in mass per mole of material. Therefore, the answer must be the only choice that does not refer to numbers of particles, i.e. **answer (B)**, which refers to grams, a unit of mass.

70. Energy is measured with the same units as _____

A. force.

B. momentum.

C. work.

D. power.

C. Work.

In SI units, energy is measured in Joules, i.e. (mass)(length squared)/(time squared). This is the same unit as is used for work. You can verify this by calculating that since work is force times distance, the units work out to be the same. Force is measured in Newtons in SI; momentum is measured in (mass)(length)/(time); power is measured in Watts (which equal Joules/second). Therefore, the **answer must be (C)**.

71. If the volume of a confined gas is increased, what happens to the pressure of the gas? You may assume that the gas behaves ideally, and that temperature and number of gas molecules remain constant.

A. The pressure increases.

B. The pressure decreases.

C. The pressure stays the same.

D. There is not enough information given to answer this question.

B. The pressure decreases.

Because we are told that the gas behaves ideally, you may assume that it follows the Ideal Gas Law, i.e. PV = nRT. This means that an increase in volume must be associated with a decrease in pressure (i.e. higher T means lower P), because we are also given that all the components of the right side of the equation remain constant. Therefore, the **answer must be (B)**.

72. A product of anaerobic respiration in animals is _____

A. carbon dioxide.

B. lactic acid.

C. oxygen.

D. sodium chloride.

B. Lactic acid.

In animals, anaerobic respiration (i.e. respiration without the presence of oxygen) generates lactic acid as a byproduct. (Note that some anaerobic bacteria generate carbon dioxide from respiration of methane, and animals generate carbon dioxide in aerobic respiration.) Oxygen is not normally a by-product of respiration, though it is a product of photosynthesis, and sodium chloride is not strictly relevant in this question. Therefore, the **answer must be (B)**. By the way, lactic acid is believed to cause muscle soreness after anaerobic weight-lifting.

TEACHER CERTIFICATION STUDY GUIDE

73. A Newton is fundamentally a measure of _____.

A. force.

B. momentum.

C. energy.

D. gravity.

A. Force.

In SI units, force is measured in Newtons. Momentum and energy each have different units, without equivalent dimensions. A Newton is one (kilogram)(meter)/(second squared), while momentum is measured in (kilgram)(meter)/(second) and energy, in Joules, is (kilogram)(meter squared)/(second squared). Although "gravity" can be interpreted as the force of gravity, i.e. measured in Newtons, fundamentally it is not required. Therefore, the **answer is (A)**.

74. Which change does *not* affect enzyme rate?

A. Increase the temperature.

B. Add more substrate.

C. Adjust the pH.

D. Use a larger cell.

D. Use a larger cell.

Temperature, chemical amounts, and pH can all affect enzyme rate. However, the chemical reactions take place on a small enough scale that the overall cell size is not relevant. Therefore, the **answer is (D)**.

75. Which of the following types of rock are made from magma?

A. Fossils.

B. Sedimentary.

C. Metamorphic.

D. Igneous.

D. Igneous.

Few fossils are found in metamorphic rock and virtually none found in igneous rocks. Igneous rocks are formed from magma and magma is so hot that any organisms trapped by it are destroyed. Metamorphic rocks are formed by high temperatures and great pressures. When fluid sediments are transformed into solid sedimentary rocks, the process is known as lithification. The **answer is (D)**.

76. Which of the following is *not* an acceptable way for a student to acknowledge sources in a laboratory report?

A. The student tells his/her teacher what sources s/he used to write the report.

B. The student uses footnotes in the text, with sources cited, but not in correct MLA format.

C. The student uses endnotes in the text, with sources cited, in correct MLA format.

D. The student attaches a separate bibliography, noting each use of sources.

A. The student tells his/her teacher what sources s/he used to write the report.

It may seem obvious, but students are often unaware that scientists need to cite all sources used. For the young adolescent, it is not always necessary to use official MLA format (though this should be taught at some point). Students may properly cite references in many ways, but these references must be in writing, with the original assignment. Therefore, the **answer is (A)**.

TEACHER CERTIFICATION STUDY GUIDE

77. Animals with a notochord or a backbone are in the phylum

A. arthropoda.

B. chordata.

C. mollusca.

D. mammalia.

B. Chordata.

The phylum arthropoda contains spiders and insects and phylum mollusca contain snails and squid. Mammalia is a class in the phylum chordata. The **answer is (B).**

78. Which of the following is a correct explanation for scientific 'evolution'?

A. Giraffes need to reach higher for leaves to eat, so their necks stretch. The giraffe babies are then born with longer necks. Eventually, there are more long-necked giraffes in the population.

B. Giraffes with longer necks are able to reach more leaves, so they eat more and have more babies than other giraffes. Eventually, there are more long-necked giraffes in the population.

C. Giraffes want to reach higher for leaves to eat, so they release enzymes into their bloodstream, which in turn causes fetal development of longer-necked giraffes. Eventually, there are more long-necked giraffes in the population.

D. Giraffes with long necks are more attractive to other giraffes, so they get the best mating partners and have more babies. Eventually, there are more long-necked giraffes in the population.

B. Giraffes with longer necks are able to reach more leaves, so they eat more and have more babies than other giraffes. Eventually, there are more long-necked giraffes in the population.

Although evolution is often misunderstood, it occurs via natural selection. Organisms with a life/reproductive advantage will produce more offspring. Over many generations, this changes the proportions of the population. In any case, it is impossible for a stretched neck (A) or a fervent desire (C) to result in a biologically mutated baby. Although there are traits that are naturally selected because of mate attractiveness and fitness (D), this is not the primary situation here, **so answer (B) is the best choice**.

MID. LEVEL SCIENCE

TEACHER CERTIFICATION STUDY GUIDE

79. Which of the following is a correct definition for 'chemical equilibrium'?

A. Chemical equilibrium is when the forward and backward reaction rates are equal. The reaction may continue to proceed forward and backward.

B. Chemical equilibrium is when the forward and backward reaction rates are equal, and equal to zero. The reaction does not continue.

C. Chemical equilibrium is when there are equal quantities of reactants and products.

D. Chemical equilibrium is when acids and bases neutralize each other fully.

A. Chemical equilibrium is when the forward and backward reaction rates are equal. The reaction may continue to proceed forward and backward.

Chemical equilibrium is defined as when the quantities of reactants and products are at a 'steady state' and are no longer shifting, but the reaction may still proceed forward and backward. The rate of forward reaction must equal the rate of backward reaction. Note that there may or may not be equal amounts of chemicals, and that this is not restricted to a completed reaction or to an acid-base reaction. Therefore, the **answer is (A)**.

80. Which of the following data sets is properly represented by a bar graph?

A. Number of people choosing to buy cars, vs. Color of car bought.

B. Number of people choosing to buy cars, vs. Age of car customer.

C. Number of people choosing to buy cars, vs. Distance from car lot to customer home.

D. Number of people choosing to buy cars, vs. Time since last car purchase.

A. Number of people choosing to buy cars, vs. Color of car bought.

A bar graph should be used only for data sets in which the independent variable is non-continuous (discrete), e.g. gender, color, etc. Any continuous independent variable (age, distance, time, etc.) should yield a scatter-plot when the dependent variable is plotted. Therefore, the **answer must be (A)**.

TEACHER CERTIFICATION STUDY GUIDE

81. In a science experiment, a student needs to dispense very small measured amounts of liquid into a well-mixed solution. Which of the following is the \best choice for his/her equipment to use?

A. Buret with Buret Stand, Stir-plate, Stirring Rod, Beaker.

B. Buret with Buret Stand, Stir-plate, Beaker.

C. Volumetric Flask, Dropper, Graduated Cylinder, Stirring Rod.

D. Beaker, Graduated Cylinder, Stir-plate.

B. Buret with Buret Stand, Stir-plate, Beaker.

The most accurate and convenient way to dispense small measured amounts of liquid in the laboratory is with a buret, on a buret stand. To keep a solution well-mixed, a magnetic stir-plate is the most sensible choice, and the solution will usually be mixed in a beaker. Although other combinations of materials could be used for this experiment, **choice (B)** is thus the simplest and best.

82. A laboratory balance is most appropriately used to measure the mass of which of the following?

A. Seven paper clips.

B. Three oranges.

C. Two hundred cells.

D. One student's elbow.

A. Seven paper clips.

Usually, laboratory/classroom balances can measure masses between approximately 0.01 gram and 1 kilogram. Therefore, answer (B) is too heavy and answer (C) is too light. Answer (D) is silly, but it is a reminder to instruct students not to lean on the balances or put their things near them. **Answer (A)**, which is likely to have a mass of a few grams, is correct in this case.

MID. LEVEL SCIENCE

83. All of the following are measured in units of length, *except* for:

A. Perimeter.

B. Distance.

C. Radius.

D. Area.

D. Area.

Perimeter is the distance around a shape; distance is equivalent to length; radius is the distance from the center (e.g. in a circle) to the edge. Area, however, is the squared-length-units measure of the size of a two-dimensional surface. Therefore, **the answer is (D)**.

84. What is specific gravity?

A. The mass of an object.

B. The ratio of the density of a substance to the density of water.

C. Density.

D. The pull of the earth's gravity on an object.

B. The ratio of the density of a substance to the density of water.

Mass is a measure of the amount of matter in an object. Density is the mass of a substance contained per unit of volume. Weight is the measure of the earth's pull of gravity on an object. The only option here is the ratio of the density of a substance to the density of water, **answer (B)**.

85. What is the most accurate description of the Water Cycle?

A. Rain comes from clouds, filling the ocean. The water then evaporates and becomes clouds again.

B. Water circulates from rivers into groundwater and back, while water vapor circulates in the atmosphere.

C. Water is conserved except for chemical or nuclear reactions, and any drop of water could circulate through clouds, rain, ground-water, and surface-water.

D. Weather systems cause chemical reactions to break water into its atoms.

C. Water is conserved except for chemical or nuclear reactions, and any drop of water could circulate through clouds, rain, ground-water, and surface-water.

All natural chemical cycles, including the Water Cycle, depend on the principle of Conservation of Mass. (For water, unlike for elements such as Nitrogen, chemical reactions may cause sources or sinks of water molecules.) Any drop of water may circulate through the hydrologic system, ending up in a cloud, as rain, or as surface- or ground-water. Although answers (A) and (B) describe parts of the water cycle, the most comprehensive and correct **answer is (C)**.

86. The scientific name *Canis familiaris* refers to the animal's _____.

A. kingdom and phylum.

B. genus and species.

C. class and species.

D. type and family.

B. Genus and species.

To answer this question, you must be aware that genus and species are the most specific way to identify an organism, and that usually the genus is capitalized and the species, immediately following, is not. Furthermore, it helps to recall that 'Canis' is the genus for dogs, or canines. Therefore, the **answer must be (B)**. If you did not remember these details, you might recall that there is no such kingdom as 'Canis,' and that there isn't a category 'type' in official taxonomy. This could eliminate answers (A) and (D).

TEACHER CERTIFICATION STUDY GUIDE

87. Members of the same animal species _____

A. look identical.

B. never adapt differently.

C. are able to reproduce with one another.

D. are found in the same location.

C. Are able to reproduce with one another.

Although members of the same animal species may look alike (A), adapt alike (B), or be found near one another (D), the only requirement is that they be able to reproduce with one another. This ability to reproduce within the group is considered the hallmark of a species. Therefore, the **answer is (C)**.

88. Which of the following is/are true about scientists?

I. Scientists usually work alone.
II. Scientists usually work with other scientists.
III. Scientists achieve more prestige from new discoveries than from replicating established results.
IV. Scientists keep records of their own work, but do not publish it for outside review.

A. I and IV only.

B. II only.

C. II and III only.

D. III and IV only.

C. II and III only.

In the scientific community, scientists nearly always work in teams, both within their institutions and across several institutions. This eliminates (I) and requires (II), leaving only **answer choices (B) and (C)**. Scientists do achieve greater prestige from new discoveries, so the answer must be (C). Note that scientists must publish their work in peer-reviewed journals, eliminating (IV) in any case.

MID. LEVEL SCIENCE

89. What is necessary for ion diffusion to occur spontaneously?

A. Carrier proteins.

B. Energy from an outside source.

C. A concentration gradient.

D. Cell flagellae.

C. A concentration gradient.

Spontaneous diffusion occurs when random motion leads particles to increase entropy by equalizing concentrations. Particles tend to move into places of lower concentration. Therefore, a concentration gradient is required, and the **answer is (C)**. No proteins (A), outside energy (B), or flagellae (D) are required for this process.

90. All of the following are considered Newton's Laws *except* for:

A. An object in motion will continue in motion unless acted upon by an outside force.

B. For every action force, there is an equal and opposite reaction force.

C. Nature abhors a vacuum.

D. Mass can be considered the ratio of force to acceleration.

C. Nature abhors a vacuum.

Newton's Laws include his law of inertia (an object in motion (or at rest) will stay in motion (or at rest) until acted upon by an outside force) (A), his law that (Force)=(Mass)(Acceleration) (D), and his equal and opposite reaction force law (B). Therefore, the **answer to this question is (C)**, because "Nature abhors a vacuum" is not one of these.

91. A cup of hot liquid and a cup of cold liquid are both sitting in a room at comfortable room temperature and humidity. Both cups are thin plastic. Which of the following is a true statement?

A. There will be fog on the outside of the hot liquid cup, and also fog on the outside of the cold liquid cup.

B. There will be fog on the outside of the hot liquid cup, but not on the cold liquid cup.

C. There will be fog on the outside of the cold liquid cup, but not on the hot liquid cup.

D. There will not be fog on the outside of either cup.

C. There will be fog on the outside of the cold liquid cup, but not on the hot liquid cup.

Fog forms on the outside of a cup when the contents of the cup are colder than the surrounding air, and the cup material is not a perfect insulator. This happens because the air surrounding the cup is cooled to a lower temperature than the ambient room, so it has a lower saturation point for water vapor. Although the humidity had been reasonable in the warmer air, when that air circulates near the colder region and cools, water condenses onto the cup's outside surface. This phenomenon is also visible when someone takes a hot shower, and the mirror gets foggy. The mirror surface is cooler than the ambient air, and provides a surface for water condensation. Furthermore, the same phenomenon is why defrosters on car windows send heat to the windows—the warmer window does not permit as much condensation. Therefore, the correct **answer is (C)**.

92. A ball rolls down a smooth hill. You may ignore air resistance. Which of the following is a true statement?

A. The ball has more energy at the start of its descent than just before it hits the bottom of the hill, because it is higher up at the beginning.

B. The ball has less energy at the start of its descent than just before it hits the bottom of the hill, because it is moving more quickly at the end.

C. The ball has the same energy throughout its descent, because positional energy is converted to energy of motion.

D. The ball has the same energy throughout its descent, because a single object (such as a ball) cannot gain or lose energy.

C. The ball has the same energy throughout its descent, because positional energy is converted to energy of motion.

The principle of Conservation of Energy states that (except in cases of nuclear reaction, when energy may be created or destroyed by conversion to mass), "Energy is neither created nor destroyed, but may be transformed." Answers (A) and (B) give you a hint in this question—it is true that the ball has more Potential Energy when it is higher, and that it has more Kinetic Energy when it is moving quickly at the bottom of its descent. However, the total sum of all kinds of energy in the ball remains constant, if we neglect 'losses' to heat/friction. Note that a single object can and does gain or lose energy when the energy is transferred to or from a different object. Conservation of Energy applies to systems, not to individual objects unless they are isolated. Therefore, the **answer must be (C)**.

TEACHER CERTIFICATION STUDY GUIDE

93. A long silver bar has a temperature of 50 degrees Celsius at one end and 0 degrees Celsius at the other end. The bar will reach thermal equilibrium (barring outside influence) by the process of heat _____.

A. conduction.

B. convection.

C. radiation.

D. phase change.

A. conduction.

Heat conduction is the process of heat transfer via solid contact. The molecules in a warmer region vibrate more rapidly, jostling neighboring molecules and accelerating them. This is the dominant heat transfer process in a solid with no outside influences. Recall, also, that convection is heat transfer by way of fluid currents; radiation is heat transfer via electromagnetic waves; phase change can account for heat transfer in the form of shifts in matter phase. The answer to this question must **therefore be (A)**.

94. _____ are cracks in the plates of the earth's crust, along which the plates move.

A. Faults

B. Ridges

C. Earthquakes

D. Volcanoes

A. Faults.

Faults are cracks in the earth's crust, and when the earth moves, an earthquake results. Faults may lead to mismatched edges of ground, forming ridges, and ground shape may also be determined by volcanoes. The answer to this question must **therefore be (A)**.

95. Fossils are usually found in _____ rock.

A. igneous.

B. sedimentary.

C. metamorphic.

D. cumulus.

B. Sedimentary

Fossils are formed by layers of dirt and sand settling around organisms, hardening, and taking an imprint of the organisms. When the organism decays, the hardened imprint is left behind. This is most likely to happen in rocks that form from layers of settling dirt and sand, i.e. sedimentary rock. Note that igneous rock is formed from molten rock from volcanoes (lava), while metamorphic rock can be formed from any rock under very high temperature and pressure changes. 'Cumulus' is a descriptor for clouds, not rocks. The best answer is **therefore (B)**.

96. Which of the following is *not* a common type of acid in 'acid rain' or acidified surface water?

A. Nitric acid.

B. Sulfuric acid.

C. Carbonic acid.

D. Hydrofluoric acid.

D. Hydrofluoric acid.

Acid rain forms predominantly from pollutant oxides in the air (usually nitrogen-based NO_x or sulfur-based SO_x), which become hydrated into their acids (nitric or sulfuric acid). Because of increased levels of carbon dioxide pollution, carbonic acid is also common in acidified surface water environments. Hydrofluoric acid can be found, but it is much less common. In general, carbon, nitrogen, and sulfur are much more prevalent in the environment than fluorine. Therefore, the **answer is (D)**.

TEACHER CERTIFICATION STUDY GUIDE

97. Which of the following is *not* true about phase change in matter?

A. Solid water and liquid ice can coexist at water's freezing point.

B. At 7 degrees Celsius, water is always in liquid phase.

C. Matter changes phase when enough energy is gained or lost.

D. Different phases of matter are characterized by differences in molecular motion.

B. At 7 degrees Celsius, water is always in liquid phase.

According to the molecular theory of matter, molecular motion determines the 'phase' of the matter, and the energy in the matter determines the speed of molecular motion. Solids have vibrating molecules that are in fixed relative positions; liquids have faster molecular motion than their solid forms, and the molecules may move more freely but must still be in contact with one another; gases have even more energy and more molecular motion. (Other phases, such as plasma, are yet more energetic.) At the 'freezing point' or 'boiling point' of a substance, both relevant phases may be present. For instance, water at zero degrees Celsius may be composed of some liquid and some solid, or all liquid, or all solid. Pressure changes, in addition to temperature changes, can cause phase changes. For example, nitrogen can be liquefied under high pressure, even though its boiling temperature is very low. Therefore, the **correct answer must be (B)**. Water may be a liquid at that temperature, but it may also be a solid, depending on ambient pressure.

98. Which of the following is the longest (largest) unit of geological time?

A. Solar Year.

B. Epoch.

C. Period.

D. Era.

D. Era.

Geological time is measured by many units, but the longest unit listed here (and indeed the longest used to describe the biological development of the planet) is the Era. Eras are subdivided into Periods, which are further divided into Epochs. Therefore, the **answer is (D)**.

MID. LEVEL SCIENCE

99. Extensive use of antibacterial soap has been found to increase the virulence of certain infections in hospitals. Which of the following might be an explanation for this phenomenon?

A. Antibacterial soaps do not kill viruses.

B. Antibacterial soaps do not incorporate the same antibiotics used as medicine.

C. Antibacterial soaps kill a lot of bacteria, and only the hardiest ones survive to reproduce.

D. Antibacterial soaps can be very drying to the skin.

C. Antibacterial soaps kill a lot of bacteria, and only the hardiest ones survive to reproduce.

All of the answer choices in this question are true statements, but the question specifically asks for a cause of increased disease virulence in hospitals. This phenomenon is due to natural selection. The bacteria that can survive contact with antibacterial soap are the strongest ones, and without other bacteria competing for resources, they have more opportunity to flourish. This problem has led to several antibiotic-resistant bacterial diseases in hospitals nation-wide. Therefore, the **answer is (C)**. However, note that answers (A) and (D) may be additional problems with over-reliance on antibacterial products.

TEACHER CERTIFICATION STUDY GUIDE

100. Which of the following is a correct explanation for astronaut 'weightlessness'?

A. Astronauts continue to feel the pull of gravity in space, but they are so far from planets that the force is small.

B. Astronauts continue to feel the pull of gravity in space, but spacecraft have such powerful engines that those forces dominate, reducing effective weight.

C. Astronauts do not feel the pull of gravity in space, because space is a vacuum.

D. Astronauts do not feel the pull of gravity in space, because black hole forces dominate the force field, reducing their masses.

A. Astronauts continue to feel the pull of gravity in space, but they are so far from planets that the force is small.

Gravity acts over tremendous distances in space (theoretically, infinite distance, though certainly at least as far as any astronaut has traveled). However, gravitational force is inversely proportional to distance squared from a massive body. This means that when an astronaut is in space, s/he is far enough from the center of mass of any planet that the gravitational force is very small, and s/he feels 'weightless'. Space is mostly empty (i.e. vacuum), and there are some black holes, and spacecraft do have powerful engines. However, none of these has the effect attributed to it in the incorrect answer choices (B), (C), or (D). The answer to this question must **therefore be (A).**

101. The theory of 'sea floor spreading' explains _____

A. the shapes of the continents.

B. how continents collide.

C. how continents move apart.

D. how continents sink to become part of the ocean floor.

C. How continents move apart.

In the theory of 'sea floor spreading', the movement of the ocean floor causes continents to spread apart from one another. This occurs because crust plates split apart, and new material is added to the plate edges. This process pulls the continents apart, or may create new separations, and is believed to have caused the formation of the Atlantic Ocean. The **answer is (C).**

102. Which of the following animals are most likely to live in a tropical rain forest?

A. Reindeer.

B. Monkeys.

C. Puffins.

D. Bears.

B. Monkeys.

The tropical rain forest biome is hot and humid, and is very fertile—it is thought to contain almost half of the world's species. Reindeer (A), puffins (C), and bears (D), however, are usually found in much colder climates. There are several species of monkeys that thrive in hot, humid climates, so **answer (B) is correct.**

103. Which of the following is *not* a type of volcano?

A. Shield Volcanoes.

B. Composite Volcanoes.

C. Stratus Volcanoes.

D. Cinder Cone Volcanoes.

C. Stratus Volcanoes.

There are three types of volcanoes. Shield volcanoes (A) are associated with non-violent eruptions and repeated lava flow over time. Composite volcanoes (B) are built from both lava flow and layers of ash and cinders. Cinder cone volcanoes (D) are associated with violent eruptions, such that lava is thrown into the air and becomes ash or cinder before falling and accumulating. **'Stratus' (C)** is a type of cloud, not volcano, so it is the correct answer to this question.

TEACHER CERTIFICATION STUDY GUIDE

104. Which of the following is *not* a property of metalloids?

A. Metalloids are solids at standard temperature and pressure.

B. Metalloids can conduct electricity to a limited extent.

C. Metalloids are found in groups 13 through 17.

D. Metalloids all favor ionic bonding.

D. Metalloids all favor ionic bonding.

Metalloids are substances that have characteristics of both metals and nonmetals, including limited conduction of electricity and solid phase at standard temperature and pressure. Metalloids are found in a 'stair-step' pattern from Boron in group 13 through Astatine in group 17. Some metalloids, e.g. Silicon, favor covalent bonding. Others, e.g. Astatine, can bond ionically. Therefore, **the answer is (D)**. Recall that metals/nonmetals/metalloids are not strictly defined by Periodic Table group, so their bonding is unlikely to be consistent with one another.

105. Which of these is a true statement about loamy soil?

A. Loamy soil is gritty and porous.

B. Loamy soil is smooth and a good barrier to water.

C. Loamy soil is hostile to microorganisms.

D. Loamy soil is velvety and clumpy.

D. Loamy soil is velvety and clumpy.

The three classes of soil by texture are: Sandy (gritty and porous), Clay (smooth, greasy, and most impervious to water), and Loamy (velvety, clumpy, and able to hold water and let water flow through). In addition, loamy soils are often the most fertile soils. Therefore, the **answer must be (D)**.

106. Lithification refers to the process by which unconsolidated sediments are transformed into _____

A. metamorphic rocks.

B. sedimentary rocks.

C. igneous rocks.

D. lithium oxide.

B. Sedimentary rocks.

Lithification is the process of sediments coming together to form rocks, i.e. sedimentary rock formation. Metamorphic and igneous rocks are formed via other processes (heat and pressure or volcano, respectively). Lithium oxide shares a word root with 'lithification' but is otherwise unrelated to this question. Therefore, the **answer must be (B)**.

107. Igneous rocks can be classified according to which of the following?

A. Texture.

B. Composition.

C. Formation process.

D. All of the above.

D. All of the above.

Igneous rocks, which form from the crystallization of molten lava, are classified according to many of their characteristics, including texture, composition, and how they were formed. Therefore, **the answer is (D)**.

TEACHER CERTIFICATION STUDY GUIDE

108. Which of the following is the most accurate definition of a nonrenewable resource?

A. A nonrenewable resource is never replaced once used.

B. A nonrenewable resource is replaced on a timescale that is very long relative to human life-spans.

C. A nonrenewable resource is a resource that can only be manufactured by humans.

D. A nonrenewable resource is a species that has already become extinct.

B. A nonrenewable resource is replaced on a timescale that is very long relative to human life-spans.

Renewable resources are those that are renewed, or replaced, in time for humans to use more of them. Examples include fast-growing plants, animals, or oxygen gas. (Note that while sunlight is often considered a renewable resource, it is actually a nonrenewable but extremely abundant resource.) Nonrenewable resources are those that renew themselves only on very long timescales, usually geologic timescales. Examples include minerals, metals, or fossil fuels. Therefore, the **correct answer is (B)**.

109. The theory of 'continental drift' is supported by which of the following?

A. The way the shapes of South America and Europe fit together.

B. The way the shapes of Europe and Asia fit together.

C. The way the shapes of South America and Africa fit together.

D. The way the shapes of North America and Antarctica fit together.

C. The way the shapes of South America and Africa fit together.

The theory of 'continental drift' states that many years ago, there was one land mass on the earth ('pangea'). This land mass broke apart via earth crust motion, and the continents drifted apart as separate pieces. This is supported by the shapes of South America and Africa, which seem to fit together like puzzle pieces if you look at a globe. Note that answer choices (A), (B), and (D) give either land masses that do not fit together, or those that are still attached to each other. Therefore, the **answer must be (C)**.

MID. LEVEL SCIENCE

110. When water falls to a cave floor and evaporates, it may deposit calcium carbonate. This process leads to the formation of which of the following?

A. Stalactites.

B. Stalagmites.

C. Fault lines.

D. Sedimentary rocks.

B. Stalagmites.

To answer this question, recall the trick to remember the kinds of crystals formed in caves. Stalactites have a 'T' in them, because they form hanging from the ceiling (resembling a 'T'). Stalagmites have an 'M' in them, because they make bumps on the floor (resembling an 'M'). Note that fault lines and sedimentary rocks are irrelevant to this question. Therefore, **the answer must be (B)**.

111. A child has type O blood. Her father has type A blood, and her mother has type B blood. What are the genotypes of the father and mother, respectively?

A. AO and BO.

B. AA and AB.

C. OO and BO.

D. AO and BB.

A. AO and BO.

Because O blood is recessive, the child must have inherited two O's—one from each of her parents. Since her father has type A blood, his genotype must be AO; likewise her mother's blood must be BO. Therefore, only **answer (A)** can be correct.

TEACHER CERTIFICATION STUDY GUIDE

112. Which of the following is the best definition for 'meteorite'?

A. A meteorite is a mineral composed of mica and feldspar.

B. A meteorite is material from outer space, that has struck the earth's surface.

C. A meteorite is an element that has properties of both metals and nonmetals.

D. A meteorite is a very small unit of length measurement.

B. A meteorite is material from outer space, that has struck the earth's surface.

Meteoroids are pieces of matter in space, composed of particles of rock and metal. If a meteoroid travels through the earth's atmosphere, friction causes burning and a "shooting star"—i.e. a meteor. If the meteor strikes the earth's surface, it is known as a meterorite. Note that although the suffix –ite often means a mineral, answer (A) is incorrect. Answer (C) refers to a 'metalloid' rather than a 'meteorite', and answer (D) is simply a misleading pun on 'meter'. Therefore, the **answer is (B)**.

113. A white flower is crossed with a red flower. Which of the following is a sign of incomplete dominance?

A. Pink flowers.

B. Red flowers.

C. White flowers.

D. No flowers.

A. Pink flowers.

Incomplete dominance means that neither the red nor the white gene is strong enough to suppress the other. Therefore both are expressed, leading in this case to the formation of pink flowers. Therefore, the **answer is (A)**.

TEACHER CERTIFICATION STUDY GUIDE

114. What is the source for most of the United States' drinking water?

A. Desalinated ocean water.

B. Surface water (lakes, streams, mountain runoff).

C. Rainfall into municipal reservoirs.

D. Groundwater.

D. Groundwater.

Groundwater currently provides drinking water for 53% of the population of the United States. (Although groundwater is often less polluted than surface water, it can be contaminated and it is very hard to clean once it is polluted. If too much groundwater is used from one area, then the ground may sink or shift, or local salt water may intrude from ocean boundaries.) The other answer choices can be used for drinking water, but they are not the most widely used. Therefore, **the answer is (D)**.

115. Which is the correct sequence of insect development?

A. Egg, pupa, larva, adult.

B. Egg, larva, pupa, adult.

C. Egg, adult, larva, pupa.

D. Pupa, egg, larva, adult.

B. Egg, larva, pupa, adult.

An insect begins as an egg, hatches into a larva (e.g. caterpillar), forms a pupa (e.g. cocoon), and emerges as an adult (e.g. moth). Therefore, the **answer is (B)**.

116. A wrasse (fish) cleans the teeth of other fish by eating away plaque. This is an example of _____ between the fish.

A. parasitism.

B. symbiosis (mutualism).

C. competition.

D. predation.

B. Symbiosis (mutualism).

When both species benefit from their interaction in their habitat, this is called 'symbiosis', or 'mutualism'. In this example, the wrasse benefits from having a source of food, and the other fish benefit by having healthier teeth. Note that 'parasitism' is when one species benefits at the expense of the other, 'competition' is when two species compete with one another for the same habitat or food, and 'predation' is when one species feeds on another. Therefore, the **answer is (B)**.

117. What is the main obstacle to using nuclear fusion for obtaining electricity?

A. Nuclear fusion produces much more pollution than nuclear fission.

B. There is no obstacle; most power plants us nuclear fusion today.

C. Nuclear fusion requires very high temperature and activation energy.

D. The fuel for nuclear fusion is extremely expensive.

C. Nuclear fusion requires very high temperature and activation energy.

Nuclear fission is the usual process for power generation in nuclear power plants. This is carried out by splitting nuclei to release energy. The sun's energy is generated by nuclear fusion, i.e. combination of smaller nuclei into a larger nucleus. Fusion creates much less radioactive waste, but it requires extremely high temperature and activation energy, so it is not yet feasible for electricity generation. Therefore, the **answer is (C)**.

118. Which of the following is a true statement about radiation exposure and air travel?

A. Air travel exposes humans to radiation, but the level is not significant for most people.

B. Air travel exposes humans to so much radiation that it is recommended as a method of cancer treatment.

C. Air travel does not expose humans to radiation.

D. Air travel may or may not expose humans to radiation, but it has not yet been determined.

A. Air travel exposes humans to radiation, but the level is not significant for most people.

Humans are exposed to background radiation from the ground and in the atmosphere, but these levels are not considered hazardous under most circumstances, and these levels have been studied extensively. Air travel does create more exposure to atmospheric radiation, though this is much less than people usually experience through dental X-rays or other medical treatment. People whose jobs or lifestyles include a great deal of air flight may be at increased risk for certain cancers from excessive radiation exposure. Therefore, the **answer is (A)**.

119. Which process(es) result(s) in a haploid chromosome number?

A. Mitosis.

B. Meiosis.

C. Both mitosis and meiosis.

D. Neither mitosis nor meiosis.

B. Meiosis.

Meiosis is the division of sex cells. The resulting chromosome number is half the number of parent cells, i.e. a 'haploid chromosome number'. Mitosis, however, is the division of other cells, in which the chromosome number is the same as the parent cell chromosome number. Therefore, the **answer is (B)**.

TEACHER CERTIFICATION STUDY GUIDE

120. Which of the following is *not* a member of Kingdom Fungi?

A. Mold.

B. Blue-green algae.

C. Mildew.

D. Mushrooms.

B. Blue-green Algae.

Mold (A), mildew (C), and mushrooms (D) are all types of fungus. Blue-green algae, however, is in Kingdom Monera. Therefore, the **answer is (B)**.

121. Which of the following organisms use spores to reproduce?

A. Fish.

B. Flowering plants.

C. Conifers.

D. Ferns.

D. Ferns.

Ferns, in Division Pterophyta, reproduce with spores and flagellated sperm. Flowering plants reproduce via seeds, and conifers reproduce via seeds protected in cones (e.g. pinecone). Fish, of course, reproduce sexually. Therefore, the **answer is (D)**.

MID. LEVEL SCIENCE

122. What is the main difference between the 'condensation hypothesis' and the 'tidal hypothesis' for the origin of the solar system?

A. The tidal hypothesis can be tested, but the condensation hypothesis cannot.

B. The tidal hypothesis proposes a near collision of two stars pulling on each other, but the condensation hypothesis proposes condensation of rotating clouds of dust and gas.

C. The tidal hypothesis explains how tides began on planets such as Earth, but the condensation hypothesis explains how water vapor became liquid on Earth.

D. The tidal hypothesis is based on Aristotelian physics, but the condensation hypothesis is based on Newtonian mechanics.

B. The tidal hypothesis proposes a near collision of two stars pulling on each other, but the condensation hypothesis proposes condensation of rotating clouds of dust and gas.

Most scientists believe the 'condensation hypothesis,' i.e. that the solar system began when rotating clouds of dust and gas condensed into the sun and planets. A minority opinion is the 'tidal hypothesis,' i.e. that the sun almost collided with a large star. The large star's gravitational field would have then pulled gases out of the sun; these gases are thought to have begun to orbit the sun and condense into planets. Because both of these hypotheses deal with ancient, unrepeatable events, neither can be tested, eliminating answer (A). Note that both 'tidal' and 'condensation' have additional meanings in physics, but those are not relevant here, eliminating answer (C). Both hypotheses are based on best guesses using modern physics, eliminating answer (D). Therefore, the **answer is (B)**.

TEACHER CERTIFICATION STUDY GUIDE

123. Which of the following units is *not* a measure of distance?

A. AU (astronomical unit).

B. Light year.

C. Parsec.

D. Lunar year.

D. Lunar year.

Although the terminology is sometimes confusing, it is important to remember that a 'light year' (B) refers to the distance that light can travel in a year. Astronomical Units (AU) (A) also measure distance, and one AU is the distance between the sun and the earth. Parsecs (C) also measure distance, and are used in astronomical measurement- they are very large, and are usually used to measure interstellar distances. A lunar year, or any other kind of year for a planet or moon, is the *time* measure of that body's orbit. Therefore, the answer to this **question is (D)**.

124. The salinity of ocean water is closest to _____.

A. 0.035 %

B. 0.35 %

C. 3.5 %

D. 35 %

C. 3.5 %

Salinity, or concentration of dissolved salt, can be measured in mass ratio (i.e. mass of salt divided by mass of sea water). For Earth's oceans, the salinity is approximately 3.5 %, or 35 parts per thousand. Note that answers (A) and (D) can be eliminated, because (A) is so dilute as to be hardly saline, while (D) is so concentrated that it would not support ocean life. Therefore, the **answer is (C)**.

125. Which of the following will not change in a chemical reaction?

A. Number of moles of products.

B. Atomic number of one of the reactants.

C. Mass (in grams) of one of the reactants.

D. Rate of reaction.

B. Atomic number of one of the reactants.

Atomic number, i.e. the number of protons in a given element, is constant unless involved in a nuclear reaction. Meanwhile, the amounts (measured in moles (A) or in grams(C)) of reactants and products change over the course of a chemical reaction, and the rate of a chemical reaction (D) may change due to internal or external processes. Therefore, the **answer is (B)**.

XAMonline, INC. 21 Orient Ave. Melrose, MA 02176

Toll Free number 800-509-4128

TO ORDER Fax 781-662-9268 OR www.XAMonline.com

CERTIFICATION EXAMINATION FOR OKLAHOMA EDUCATORS - CEOE - 2007

PO#   Store/School:

Address 1:

Address 2 (Ship to other):
City, State Zip

Credit card number ____-____-____-____   expiration _____
EMAIL _____
PHONE   FAX

13# ISBN 2007	TITLE	Qty	Retail	Total
978-1-58197-781-3	CEOE OSAT Advanced Mathematics Field 11			
978-1-58197-775-2	CEOE OSAT Art Sample Test Field 02			
978-1-58197-780-6	CEOE OSAT Biological Sciences Field 10			
978-1-58197-776-9	CEOE OSAT Chemistry Field 04			
978-1-58197-778-3	CEOE OSAT Earth Science Field 08			
978-1-58197-794-3	CEOE OSAT Elementary Education Fields 50-51			
978-1-58197-795-0	CEOE OSAT Elementary Education Fields 50-51 Sample Questions			
978-1-58197-777-6	CEOE OSAT English Field 07			
978-1-58197-779-0	CEOE OSAT Family and Consumer Sciences Field 09			
978-1-58197-786-8	CEOE OSAT French Sample Test Field 20			
978-1-58197-798-1	CEOE OGET Oklahoma General Education Test 074			
978-1-58197-792-9	CEOE OSAT Library-Media Specialist Field 38			
978-1-58197-787-5	CEOE OSAT Middle Level English Field 24			
978-1-58197-789-9	CEOE OSAT Middle Level Science Field 26			
978-1-58197-790-5	CEOE OSAT Middle Level Social Studies Field 27			
978-1-58197-788-2	CEOE OSAT Middle Level-Intermediate Mathematics Field 25			
978-1-58197-791-2	CEOE OSAT Mild Moderate Disabilities Field 29			
978-1-58197-782-0	CEOE OSAT Physical Education-Health-Safety Field 12			
978-1-58197-783-7	CEOE OSAT Physics Sample Test Field 14			
978-1-58197-793-6	CEOE OSAT Principal Common Core Field 44			
978-1-58197-796-7	CEOE OPTE Oklahoma Professional Teaching Examination Fields 75-76			
978-1-58197-784-4	CEOE OSAT Reading Specialist Field 15			
978-1-58197-785-1	CEOE OSAT Spanish Field 19			
978-1-58197-797-4	CEOE OSAT U.S. & World History Field 17			
			SUBTOTAL	
FOR PRODUCT PRICES GO TO WWW.XAMONLINE.COM			Ship	$8.25
			TOTAL	

www.ingramcontent.com/pod-product-compliance
Lightning Source LLC
Chambersburg PA
CBHW080539300426
44111CB00017B/2796